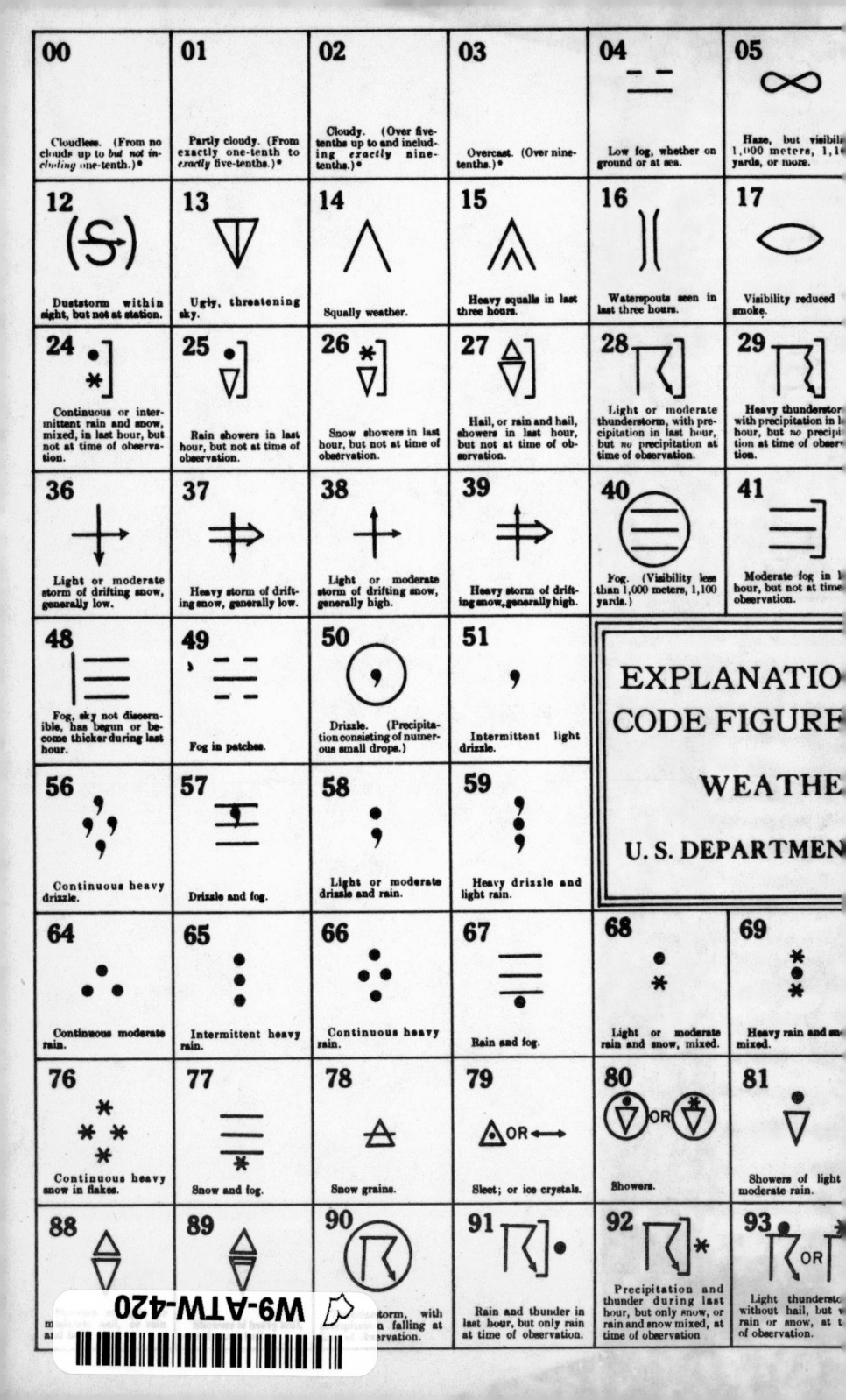

00	Cloudless. (From no clouds up to *but not including one-tenth*.)*
01	Partly cloudy. (From exactly one-tenth to *exactly* five-tenths.)*
02	Cloudy. (Over five-tenths up to and including *exactly* nine-tenths.)*
03	Overcast. (Over nine-tenths.)*
04	Low fog, whether on ground or at sea.
05	Haze, but visibility 1,000 meters, 1,1.. yards, or more.
12	Duststorm within sight, but not at station.
13	Ugly, threatening sky.
14	Squally weather.
15	Heavy squalls in last three hours.
16	Waterspouts seen in last three hours.
17	Visibility reduced smoke.
24	Continuous or intermittent rain and snow, mixed, in last hour, but not at time of observation.
25	Rain showers in last hour, but not at time of observation.
26	Snow showers in last hour, but not at time of observation.
27	Hail, or rain and hail, showers in last hour, but not at time of observation.
28	Light or moderate thunderstorm, with precipitation in last hour, but *no* precipitation at time of observation.
29	Heavy thunderstorm with precipitation in la.. hour, but *no* precipita tion at time of observ..
36	Light or moderate storm of drifting snow, generally low.
37	Heavy storm of drift ing snow, generally low.
38	Light or moderate storm of drifting snow, generally high.
39	Heavy storm of drift ing snow, generally high.
40	Fog. (Visibility less than 1,000 meters, 1,100 yards.)
41	Moderate fog in la.. hour, but not at time observation.
48	Fog, sky not discern ible, has begun or be come thicker during last hour.
49	Fog in patches.
50	Drizzle. (Precipita tion consisting of numer ous small drops.)
51	Intermittent light drizzle.
56	Continuous heavy drizzle.
57	Drizzle and fog.
58	Light or moderate drizzle and rain.
59	Heavy drizzle and light rain.
64	Continuous moderate rain.
65	Intermittent heavy rain.
66	Continuous heavy rain.
67	Rain and fog.
68	Light or moderate rain and snow, mixed.
69	Heavy rain and sn.. mixed.
76	Continuous heavy snow in flakes.
77	Snow and fog.
78	Snow grains.
79	Sleet; or ice crystals.
80	Showers.
81	Showers of light moderate rain.
88	
89	
90	
91	Rain and thunder in last hour, but only rain at time of observation.
92	Precipitation and thunder during last hour, but only snow, or rain and snow mixed, at time of observation
93	Light thunderstor.. without hail, with .. rain or snow, at .. of observation.

EXPLANATIO...
CODE FIGURE...

WEATHE...

U. S. DEPARTMEN...

WIND, STORM and RAIN

The Story of Weather

FOR ALISON

*with love and thanks for her insist-
ence that these pages tell a story.*

Preface

MOTHER nature provides inspiration for poems, songs and stories when she brings about the great variety of manifestations which she produces in her weather factories. Some of the weather coming off these meteorological production lines would make the subject of a complete, full-length novel—where air mass meets air mass, and a bit of temperature is mixed with a spot of moisture and a dash of atmospheric pressure, all stirred together by a wind of two to six on the Beaufort scale.

Take tornadoes, for instance, which spring into being suddenly, become vicious spinning whirlpools of destruction within the twinkling of an eyelash, create feats of havoc miraculous in their cruelty and then blow themselves out as quickly as they were formed. The very mechanics of such a concentrated storm are so interesting and mysterious that they have challenged students of meteorology everywhere to solve their mysteries so that some day the occurrence of these small but wicked twisters may be predicted with some sort of exactness.

The weather's changes are such that few individuals can escape their effects, as one type of air replaces another in conflicts that follow an irregular but rhythmic pattern. Some people are scarcely aware how the weather does continually influence them in one way or another, and they go about their daily tasks without bothering about the daily forecast or caring to cast an eye skyward to watch the changing meteorological scene. Others, however, are closely concerned because some personal problem is related to the weather's changing tempo or because their very business operations depend in large measure on what the weather is now or will be tomorrow.

The United States Weather Bureau endeavors to carry out its responsibility, as a Government agency, of conducting organized research in the field of meteorology, of establishing weather reporting stations on land, on sea, and in the air, of arranging for the efficient collection of weather reports so that the weather's changes can be studied by forecasters in all the forecast centers, and of maintaining forecasting and meteorological service centers from which weather advisories can be issued for public use.

But from there on it becomes the responsibility of the person who needs such advice, concerning the present or future weather, to use each forecast and advisory so as to obtain the best practical advantage from it. To do this, he should become familiar with the development of the weather and the way it changes, so that he can properly evaluate the information supplied by the Weather Bureau. He will also find it helpful to know what is available in the way of weather history or climatology, since a study of what has happened in the past is sometimes as valuable as what can be expected from a prediction as to the immediate future. This is especially true when long-term planning is necessary.

In this book, *Wind, Storm and Rain,* Denning Miller has presented the basic, interesting facts about the weather, linking them with other related scientific pursuits so that anyone reading it will enjoy the experience of learning, easily and pleasantly, how Mother Nature sets up the air-mass machinery to produce this thing called weather. It is not a textbook in any sense of the word, but a book written to give the average citizen an opportunity to peek behind the scenes of the weather's dramatic show.

Ernest J. Christie
Meteorologist in Charge
United States Weather Bureau, New York

CONTENTS

I. THE AIR WE BREATHE 3
The nature of the atmosphere and how it makes life possible

II. FROM GREENLAND'S ICY MOUNTAINS 20
How the air moves about the world

III. THE LITTLE WHEEL RUNS BY FAITH 36
Air masses and how they are bred

IV. SAY NOT THE STRUGGLE NAUGHT AVAILETH 50
Fronts and frontal storms

V. WATCHING THE CLOUDS GO BY 68
How the clouds form and what they are called

VI. THE WIND BLOWETH WHERE IT LISTETH 84
How winds adjust the atmospheric pressure

VII. THE WILD BLUE YONDER 98
The air aloft and the jet stream

VIII. WHAT A BEAUTIFUL BELT, SAID ALICE 113
Weather within the tropics. Hurricanes

IX. BRING OUT THE CHART 127
Weather maps and what they tell

X. WHAT OF THE NIGHT? 147
How to forecast the weather

GLOSSARY 167

INDEX 173

CONTENTS

ILLUSTRATIONS

1. General Circulation of the Atmosphere   23

2. A Warm Front   55

3. A Cold Front   56

4. Development of a Cyclonic Storm   62

5. Occluding Front   65

6. An Occluded Front   66

7. Cloud Photographs
   Following page   82
       I. Cirrus
       II. Cirrostratus
       III. Cirrocumulus
       IV. Altocumulus
       V. Altostratus above. Fog and Stratus below
       VI. Nimbostratus, thinning to Altostratus
          towards the horizon
       VII. Stratocumulus
       VIII. Cumulus in various stages of development

8. Weather Maps of April 3, 4, 5, and 6, 1952 at
   1:30 P.M. E.S.T.   140-143

9. Weather Maps of April 12, 13, 14, and 15, 1952
   at 1:30 P.M. E.S.T.   160-163

WIND, STORM and RAIN

The Story of Weather

CHAPTER I

The Air We Breathe

I

THE weather, it is fair to say, has been the topic of more insipid conversation, the origin of more poor jokes and the source of more minor disappointment than probably any other subject. To most people it is an object of the most immediate daily interest. And yet of its simple fundamentals they are almost completely ignorant.

This, on the practical level, is certainly a pity. Planning for business or pleasure would proceed with more confidence and less frustration if a few facts of weather wisdom were only understood and appreciated. This information, as the servicemen who were taught a necessary minimum of meteorology will agree, is neither overly technical nor excessively complicated. In fact many a flier or sailor, now on inactive service, will maintain that this knowledge, acquired in wartime haste and tested about the far corners of the world, has turned out, at home and in peacetime, to be a source of unexpected pleasure and constant enjoyment.

The reason is no doubt simple. It is not hard to think of an animal as a creature of its environment, but it is sometimes forgotten how it also is held hostage to its heredity. The years during which man has lived in city or town, engaging in urban occupations, are but a short second in relative time as compared

3

to the long days when he lived upon the land, hunting or fishing, tending his flocks or raising a rough field of grain.

A garden in the backyard, a rod or gun in the attic, a small craft turning quietly at anchor, each is a means of satisfying an urge that has come down to us from ancestors in uncounted numbers, in comparison with the few generations who have trodden the pavements to enter factory or office building. Modern man, living so predominantly indoors where steam heat or air conditioning tempers the daily impact of the weather, may pass his life largely unaware of the deep-seated, instinctive interest lying hidden somewhere in the inherited recollection which is part of all our subconscious minds.

Breaking through the thin veneer of civilization and education, these emotions come clearly to the surface when nature assumes one of her moods of violence. When a storm strikes, as a blizzard's white blanket deepens, where the tornado sweeps destruction across Kansas or a hurricane brings devastation to New England, people appear at their best.

Calm in the face of the danger, but stimulated by the drama of the spectacle, clear-thinking and forceful as each emergency arises, but gay and cheerful as if going to a wedding, unexpectedly brave and universally co-operative, folk who have lived through flood or storm or forest fire tap hidden resources of strength and vitality inherited from ancestors who had faced a succession of similar disasters down the uncounted years of prehistoric time.

Yet this is only a part of the weather's fascinating story. Armies have won empires, but so also has the discovery of a prevailing wind. The Arabs and Turks, for example, were in succession bleeding Europe white, until a band of intrepid Portuguese finally found their way around Africa and into the Indian Ocean, to cut the economic sinews which enabled the Moslem state to wage war.

The hold of these first Europeans on the treasure house of

4

the Indies, however, was brief. Dutch sailors, who came after them, learned in the next hundred years to stand boldly out into the southern ocean from their new post on the Cape of Good Hope. There in the Roaring Forties they found western winds which drove their sturdier ships directly across a quarter of the girth of the world. Here at the longitude of Java they turned north, and skirting the treacherous coast of western Australia, let the trade winds carry them to the fabulous islands of spice.

As compared to the more direct route across the Indian Ocean with its shifting airs, below the Bay of Bengal with its wicked equinoctial storms, this longer southern circuit cut almost half the time for a voyage from the Cape to Sunda Straits. It won for the Dutch in the seventeenth century the eastern empire, which they held for three hundred years and only recently surrendered.

Particularly for Americans, whose brief tenure of the mastery of the sea was ended a hundred years ago, should the way in which the winds blow about the world be a matter of pride and interest. Many of us know of Nathaniel Bowditch who perfected the art and science of navigation, of Donald McKay who designed the greatest of the clipper ships, but few have ever heard of Matthew Fontaine Maury. Lamed by the explosion of a gun in 1839, this young naval officer's enthusiasm for determining the winds and currents of all the oceans led to the first international conference on hydrography and oceanography at Brussels in 1853. At this meeting modern meteorology was born.

For seventy-five years prior to this date, however, the skippers whose home ports ranged from Salem to Baltimore had been carefully collecting the same data. During this three quarters of a century such information remained a closely guarded commercial secret, since it was securing for American owners the prime cargoes of the world and rapidly driving their British competitors to overhaul completely the design of their ships, the nature of their sail-plans and the quality of their seamanship.

As in the case of the Polynesians, the currents of the oceans and the trend of the prevailing winds may well have guided across the seas migrations of primitive peoples just as extensive as the great eruptions of races that are recorded as having occurred on land. But the span of the human race comprises only a short instant as compared to the aeons of time in the history of the world. Here weather and climate have been intimately linked with all geologic change. In no merely paradoxical sense it is true to say that the story told by the sedimentary rocks was first written in the sky among the clouds, by the winds, the rain and the sheets of glacial ice, which for intermediate periods moved down from the poles.

II

Life, no matter how mysteriously it may have first arisen, is now only maintained on earth by the energy emitted by the incandescent sun. The solar radiation is transformed within the earth's atmosphere and at the earth's surface into heat. Protecting all living things from the terrible cold of empty space, a blanket of mixed gases rises hundreds of miles above our heads. But this gaseous envelope is much more than a simple protective covering; it acts as well as a filter, a ceiling and as a most excellent mechanism for distributing about the globe the heat received from the sun.

In a very real sense man exists in an enormous greenhouse whose roof circles the world at an altitude of some six to ten miles. The rest of the atmosphere, of course, stretches away to vastly greater distances, providing sufficient friction to burn up high overhead most of the cosmic material which we see as shooting stars. Matters of great scientific interest occur in its outer reaches, but curiously enough, and fortunately too, all the natural manifestations that we know as weather are held down within a shallow shell.

Actually it is astonishing that the heat which reaches the earth is not promptly dissipated back into outer space. Air, after being heated at the earth's surface, might naturally be expected to rise to the thin fringes of the atmosphere where all its warmth would be lost. If this were so, life as we know it could not exist. But luckily for us certain of the rays that the sun sends us have a special affinity for the oxygen that comprises a fifth of the air we breathe. Invisible to the human eye, these rays lie in the spectrum beyond the darkest violet. Their radiant energy, more powerful than the tropic sun, is lethal to most living things.

The principal actors on the meteorological stage are oxygen, dust, and water vapor. Of the three, oxygen, since it is essential to life, is logically the first to be introduced. All animals existing on land or sea must have this gas entering their lungs regularly and continuously. This is oxygen's vital function at the earth's surface, where each of its chemical particles, or molecules, is formed of two atoms of this element. But high overhead it serves a prior and equally necessary purpose. Here it absorbs the deadly ultraviolet rays which then act to add a third atom to the usual two and thus produce a different gas called ozone.

This act of absorption occurs through many miles of the atmosphere's depth in what is called the *stratosphere*. Here ozone continuously picks up the energy of additional motion as its triangular molecule interrupts the earthward flow of the sun's most killing rays. As a result the temperature of the stratosphere remains much the same and does not fall off as one moves outward into space. This uniformity in the thermometer's reading acts like an enormous hand holding down the lower air, which otherwise would escape upwards, releasing the sun's warmth into the killing cold of interstellar space.

It is often a confusing fact that there are generally two ways of putting a thing. Air will rise, we know, when it is warmed, but it would be just as true to say that a parcel of such gas will move upward if the atmosphere around it is colder than it is. It is the existence of this latter situation which is prevented by the stratosphere's uniform temperature of some sixty to eighty degrees below zero. This to be sure is cold, but equally low readings are recorded on earth. More importantly any column or mass of air, rising or lifting from the earth's surface, grows naturally colder in its ascent, until at the base of the cold stratosphere it finds above it layers as warm or warmer than itself. Then it can rise no further.

This is the final trick of oxygen, the vital gas that supports life. In our lungs, fireplaces and furnaces it combines with carbon to supply us with the internal heat that energizes our existence. Next it intercepts, miles overhead, a band of radiation which otherwise would kill us. And finally, in the acceptance of these rays it picks up the motion which holds down the warmed and lifting air below it, whose motions we see and know as Weather.

III

Meteorology is primarily a science that concerns movings and shiftings, alterations and adjustments. The shallow skin within which all this is confined is called the *troposphere*, from the Greek word meaning "change." As the clouds roll away or the rains come down, here is a stage on which a never-ending sequence of meteorological events moves overhead, inspiring or interrupting man's daily doings. Where down the ages he has attempted to interpret these matters by primitive rite, sacrifice or superstition, we have today the scientist with his vast knowledge and his assemblage of shining instruments. In some ways we are not much better off.

Despite the power of modern education, an understanding of physical facts is generally associated with immediate personal experience. Pressure is the amount of air in a tire; heat is the luxury of an open fire; evaporation is the chill of a sweat-soaked shirt. In these terms natural phenomena are relative to some assemblage of objects, more homely to be sure, but essentially much the same as those in a college laboratory. Condensation forms on a bathroom window; a cooling cup sticks to a linoleum drainboard; a cat's fur emits sparks on a dry cold day.

The weather shifts and changes in tune to facts like these, observed by everyone in such pieces of homely apparatus. But in the mixed gases of the troposphere there is unfortunately no such ready frame of reference. With the exception of the clouds and the rain which in due course may fall, all is gas, moving invisibly through other gases. From the earth's undulating surface to the underside of the stratosphere there is no tangible background for man's ideas to tie to. Only in its moods of violence and otherwise just by the wind on our cheek, do we know much that is physically revealing about the air we breathe.

Appropriately enough therefore the cycle on which so much of the weather depends begins with an act of disappearance. From the warm seas and forests of the tropics, from the woods and fields of the middle latitudes and even from the snow and ice about the poles, water is constantly rising into the atmosphere. This process is evaporation by which a restlessly moving molecule occasionally darts free of the tight pull exerted on it by its neighbors.

As sugar or salt will dissolve invisibly in a glass of clear liquid, so water disappears into the other transparent gases of the air. *Water vapor,* to give it its technical name, can only

9

amount to a tiny fraction of the atmosphere's total, before it must return to its source or start condensing into fog or cloud. But imperceptible to the eye and inconsiderable in amount, here is the active agent that produces the thunderstorm and the hurricane, that moves indeed through all the changes in the weather.

A cycle like a circle is a hard thing to describe. Any place on its rim, taken as a beginning, is wholly arbitrary. The thing exists as a whole, an effect in one phase being the cause in the next. So it is with the water cycle and its effects on the weather. Following its evaporation as water vapor, water returns to sight as cloud or fog and eventually comes back to earth as rain or snow. But the change of solid or liquid into transparent gas is not simply an act of disappearance.

When a molecule shoots clear of its parent lake or ocean, it commits at the same time a skillful piece of robbery. Secreted somewhere about its person, stowed away in the electrical forces that hold it together, it absconds with a large amount of the heat belonging to the brothers which it leaves behind. Here is a scientific fact universally appreciated. It is not, we constantly remind ourselves, the heat, but the humidity. When the air is dry, the moisture of our bodies departs readily, leaving us the cooler by its theft of heat. But when the atmosphere is already full of water vapor our perspiration clings to our shirt, unable to disappear into the surrounding surfeited gases.

The measure of our comfort in this respect is the *relative humidity*, relative because hot air can hold more moisture than cold. When this figure rises to a hundred per cent, a balance is struck between the air and any wet surface with which it is in contact. Then as many molecules of water are returning to their liquid home as are leaving it and disappearing into the air. But below that point any breeze or current is beneficial in removing the evaporated water vapor and replacing it by new air into which more of our body's moisture can be absorbed.

In the depths and reaches of the atmosphere this stolen heat is an active force. Like a pickpocket in the hands of the police, the invisible water vapor is forced to give up its purloined energy when in due course it is changed back into fog or cloud. In this transformation, its partner is a host of countless motes. These comprise the dust of the atmosphere, existing in such quantities that they occur at the center of each tiny water droplet or infant snowflake which in total make up the clouds.

IV

The set rules of high school physics tend to picture Nature as a heavy, unattractive, stolid wench. The rules are certainly right enough, but what such teaching is apt to omit is the uncertain, coy, moody or imponderable way in which she often chooses to apply her own regulations. If a reaction is unexpected, it is not because the laws of physics have been abrogated; it is because more factors have been involved than the observer has anticipated.

For example, when a parcel of air in cooling reaches a hundred per cent humidity it is said to have reached the *dew point*. This is an excellently descriptive term as long as it is understood that the evening dew is water vapor which has condensed on some assemblage of objects, such as the grass, an automobile or a spider's web. In the air these objects are the atmospheric dust.

It is almost impossible to believe that for every liquid drop and tiny snowflake making up the clouds there was first a solid mote of matter for the water to form on. Yet if these infinitesimal particles are not present, water vapor will promptly violate the textbook rules and sulkily refuse to reappear as

11

condensation until it has built itself up to five or six hundred per cent of relative humidity.

Occasionally a storm will sweep a portion of the sky bare of such dust. If in perfectly clear weather the air-traveler observes water or ice forming on his plane, he can be sure that he is passing through a patch of such supersaturated air. Before the days of adequate de-icers a pilot was always careful to stay, if he could, below the freezing level when entering one of those areas where Nature seems to deny one of her own principles.

Dust to the average housewife means coarse dirt, only to be eradicated by the daily application of hard work. But the impalpable stuff of the atmosphere is even finer than the minute dots which dance down a shaft of sunlight. Lifted from desert and dried field, consisting of the salt contained in a single drop of sea spray, including the pollen brushed from a bee's wing and the smoke of factory or cottage, it is carried by the winds around the world and up to the base of the stratosphere. At earliest dawn or late dusk it tints the sky red and purple, coloring in daylight the distant hills a deepening blue. Otherwise it remains as invisible as the water vapor with which it acts in the formation of clouds.

The development of new ideas is aided by comparison; understanding grows best with the assignment of similarity or difference. In the third and final phase of the atmosphere's water cycle a succession of differences is essential. This is the delicate and climactic process by which the evaporated water vapor, having changed into cloud, returns to earth as rain or snow. Although a Scotch mist or fine drizzle can at times be wrung out of a single cloud, steady rain or heavy shower can only descend as a result of one of those contrasts by which Nature upsets her otherwise evenly balanced forces.

The initial difference concerns the nature of the atmospheric dust. Right up to the stratosphere, scientists have found pollen and other vegetable matter. Interesting as this fact may be to the botanist, it is of little importance to the meteorologist. Water has no liking for such plant material, which comprises only an unimportant fraction of the air's dust. A considerably larger part consists of the sand and clay whirled aloft by the winds from desert and field. The coarser grains return to earth, but the finest are lifted bodily to the base of the stratosphere.

Their size is microscopic, comparable to the minute particles which we see as smoke. One major source, indeed, is from erupting volcanoes. When Krakatau in the Dutch East Indies exploded in 1883, the whole world enjoyed sunsets of superb brilliance due to the fine ash supplied to the atmosphere. In the past history of the world, eras of volcanic violence must have fed tremendous quantities of such nuclei to the air, and these in turn could well have played a major role in the climatic changes of geologic time.

A quite different kind of dust is derived from the sea. The winds, continually lashing the oceans, lift spray and spindrift into the air. There evaporation removes the water, leaving the salt. This, like the sandy particles from desert and volcano, has an avid affinity for water.

As a result, near the seashore distant objects on a still, warm day will sometimes seem much closer than usual. At a relative humidity of seventy per cent some of the invisible molecules will have started to leave the air. As the first thin, invisible layers of water form on such dust, the light rays from objects some miles away are no longer scattered but merely bent. The blue haze that one's mind associates with distance is no longer there, so that when the horizon seems unnaturally close, it is often a sign of rain, of a change for the worse in tomorrow's weather.

This partnership between water and dust is of two kinds. The water vapor simply clings to the sand, but dissolves the

13

salt. In our latitudes one does not have to ascend many thousands of feet before the temperature drops to freezing. During the war the weather planes of the Air Force often took along the ice cream to be frozen for the men's mess. And there are stories of champagne being similarly chilled for use at the Officers' Club.

Be that as it may, this is the level above which many of our clouds take shape. Here water vapor will sublime on the sand to ice, this being the lovely scientific verb for the direct change of a gas to a solid. The salt, however, will form with the first condensing molecules of water a saline solution, which like sea water must be chilled below thirty-two degrees before freezing. The meteorologists therefore have different names for the two sorts of active dust. Those particles which will dissolve are termed *condensation nuclei;* those which can not are called *sublimation nuclei.*

Man is always monkeying with nature, sometimes for practical reasons, at others urged on simply by the innate curiosity which is at the root of much scientific interest. An ability to produce rain during periods of drought would be of inestimable value to civilization. To the meteorologist, however, the more interesting point on which the rain makers have thrown new light is the exact conditions under which they have successfully forced a cloud to surrender some of its suspended moisture.

For this purpose they use a substitute form of sublimation nuclei, or else seed the cloud with particles that act like tiny ice crystals. For the first, a smoke of silver iodide is employed; for the second, the dry ice of carbon dioxide. Whichever method is used, nothing much happens if the cloud is composed of minute snowflakes or is warmer than the temperature at which fresh water will freeze. But if it is in the in-between state with its particles liquid but colder than the freezing temperature of fresh water, then it can be made to destroy itself,

14

its moisture concentrating and building up into snow or rain.

The difference between gaseous water vapor, liquid water and solid ice is what the physicists call a difference in state. In the middle and northern latitudes such a difference in the particles comprising the clouds is the principal cause of precipitation. However, a sufficient contrast in temperature can likewise do the trick, and this is the way in which the heavy rains of the tropics generally occur. But for clouds of different state or contrasting temperature to come together and intermingle, the air itself must do its part.

The atmosphere is the stage on which water and dust put on their act. But they are indeed really marionettes, whose entrances and exits are manipulated by an unseen force. Originating in the heart of the sun's atoms, the hand that pulls the strings is of all things the most vital and the least tangible. Puppets to its pull, the clouds form and the air moves above the earth under the continual impulsion of the force of heat.

V

Along the Nile, as elsewhere about the world after the harvests are in, the natives burn off their brush and trash. Generally the result is much the same as when we start in autumn a fire of fallen leaves. Sometimes, however, at this time of year the desert air, exceptionally hot at the surface, is unusually cold up aloft. Then the little eddies of smoke will grow and expand into a series of mounting whirlpools of leaves and dust. The result is a sort of dry thunderstorm, towering thousands of feet skywards.

Heat is here the force that has triggered the rising currents. Only a little is needed where the air, lying hot over baking fields and desert, grows cooler comparatively rapidly in its successive upper layers. Where the temperature falls off more slowly with altitude, more of this energy is required. For ex-

15

ample, many a great forest fire has bred the thunderstorms which have helped in its eventual quenching.

The air over the Sahara is about the driest found anywhere about our planet. To the south, however, over the warm seas and steaming jungles of the equator, the surface layers have generally absorbed nearly all the water vapor they can pick up by evaporation. If such moisture-laden air is then heated, it will start upwards like the smoke from the Egyptians' fire. As it ascends, it will shortly reach a level where its invisible water vapor will change into visible cloud. As this condensation takes place, the heat originally stolen from swamp or ocean must be surrendered. The mounting current now begins to manufacture within itself additional energy to aid it in its further upward course.

During the war this natural property of moist air was a great help to our fliers in the Pacific. The warmth of the morning sun upon even a tiny atoll or spit of sand was sufficient to heat the air lying above it, so that it would start rising, to form as the day advanced billowing cumulus cloud. These atmospheric beacons could be seen long before each small island and its rough airstrip could themselves be identified. Each dot of land—by its ability to supply more heat to the air above it than could the sea around it—would on a clear day raise aloft a beckoning pillar of cloud.

It would be much easier for the average man or woman to visualize such rising currents if the atmosphere was all at the same density. Instead, like the low man of a human pyramid, the air near the earth's surface carries the weight of all the atmospheric levels above it. As a result our gaseous envelope grows progressively thinner as one moves away from the earth's surface. Indeed at only 18,000 feet half of its weight is below us, the remainder stretching out mile after mile into space.

Under these circumstances it is helpful to remember that

all matter moves. Motion, not rest, is the natural state. In a solid or liquid the individual particles of matter are kept close together by strong, connecting bonds which hold them to short and limited paths. In a gas, however, every infinitesimal molecule is moving freely, each contact with its fellows consisting of an elastic collision from which it rebounds like a perfect billiard ball.

A child burning his hand on a hot stove learns to sense heat and as he grows older tests the temperatures of his bath with a gently probing foot. In the compact state of solid or liquid, heat is directly related to the average speed of the individual molecules. But in a gas the situation is more complicated, the thermometer's reading depending on the number of particles striking the bulb as well as on their average velocity.

When some part of the air is warmed, its molecules are accelerated, their speedier motion causing them to spread out slightly. Being now less dense than the cooler gas around them, they start to rise. But as such a heated parcel ascends, the atmosphere at each new level presses in upon it less firmly. As a result of this trick of gravity, the mounting column of air expands and in expanding grows cooler.

Such an ascending shaft of air plays a dramatic part in producing rounded cumulus cloud or angry thunderstorm. But after it has received its initial supply of heat at the earth's surface, its dynamic appearance is in fact misleading. It can do only one thing and do it in but two ways. As long as its water vapor stays invisible, it will cool off at five and a half degrees for every thousand feet of its ascent. Once it reaches the level where it becomes cold enough for its transparent moisture to change into cloud, however, the stolen heat given up by this process reduces its rate of cooling to three degrees for each thousand feet of upward climb.

How far it rises depends, to be sure, partly on its initial supply of heat. Indeed if you heat up enough of the atmospheric gas and heat it hot enough, you can drive it right up to the base of the stratosphere. But under ordinary circumstances the ascent of any column or parcel of air depends not so much on its own temperature as on the way the atmosphere is stacked up above it.

The atmospheric levels which encourage a heated parcel of air to move upward in an ascending current are called unstable. Flying through them is apt to be rough and uncomfortable, as your aircraft enters and leaves each area where an invisible column of warmer air is mounting upwards. Air that grows colder aloft at five and a half degrees per thousand feet is called *absolutely unstable,* since any local heating will immediately start a current rising dynamically upward.

Rarely except over the hot deserts does the air grow colder with altitude at this high rate. More commonly the drop in temperature will lie below this figure but above three degrees Fahrenheit. Such air is called *conditionally unstable,* since any ascending current must first be heated sufficiently to drive it up to the condensation level. There its water vapor starts its change into cloud. And the consequent return of purloined heat will thereafter keep this air warmer than the new levels into which it will continue to rise.

Unstable air is characteristic of the tropics and, in our latitudes, of the summer months. As during the day the sun mounts higher in the heavens, heating the ground and the air's lower layers, the lapse rate, as it is termed, at which the air's temperature decreases with altitude, grows greater. The atmosphere's instability tends to rise. But as the sun sets and its warmth departs, the air reverses this tendency and becomes more quiet and stable as the earth's surface radiates away its daytime heat.

Stable air is air that grows slowly colder aloft, at a rate less than three degrees per thousand feet. At the poles, for example, during the Arctic night, the surface temperature is not much different from that at the base of the stratosphere. Under such conditions of atmospheric stability any local heating can only move a parcel of air up to the levels where its supply of warmth is used up. Beyond that it can ascend no further. Thus on a still January morning the smoke from our chimneys can often be seen rising vertically a few hundred feet and then streaming sharply sideways like a banner in the light air.

Stable air is characteristic of the polar regions, of the winter and the night. But all the year round and in every latitude the moving winds are constantly rearranging the air aloft. The clouds they drive before them tell much about how the temperature of these upper levels is adjusted. When the air is stable and heavy, the clouds will be level and even. When, on the other hand, they appear round and puffy, the temperature aloft is dropping off more rapidly with altitude. When finally the rolling cumulus begins to build up and to threaten a thunderstorm to follow, the air is highly unstable, growing sufficiently cold throughout enough of its great depth to encourage the development of these towering thermal currents.

The solar heat that lifts some column or shaft of air is the same force which on a grander scale drives the winds about the world. Coy and unpredictable as the weather's design must often seem to us, its immediate vagaries are woven within a global pattern by which the air is warmed at the equator and flows thence north or south, eventually to cool and sink above the poles.

CHAPTER II

From Greenland's Icy Mountains

I

IN the prosperous days between the War of 1812 and the Mexican War in 1848, the United States was the leading maritime nation of the world. In tonnage afloat, England somewhat surpassed the young republic; but in navigation, seamanship and all phases of naval design and architecture the erstwhile colonies were far ahead of the mother country. In a decade and a half, the lure of new lands beyond the Mississippi, the clash of ideas that became the Civil War and the rapid change from wood and sail to steel and steam, all combined to lose America its maritime supremacy; for a hundred years thereafter the nation's ambitions turned inland.

When gold was discovered in California, the first of these factors was beginning to operate. Young men from Baltimore to Boston were no longer shipping out as seamen or supercargoes, secure in the expectation of becoming master or mate while still in their twenties. Instead they were moving with the advancing western frontier, anticipating the later advice of a famous New York publisher. And yet, although the crews were being increasingly drawn from seagoing immigrants, the craft they sailed climaxed fifty years of American nautical design.

The famous clipper ships were things of beauty and perfection, attaining speeds that the new steam vessels were for many years unable to equal. Stemming from the tea trade with China, their design was concentrated on making the fastest voyage, carrying passengers, mail and expensive freight to the new Eldorado in California. Like so many specialized products they disappeared when this particular need ceased to exist, but for a brief span of fifteen years, from 1845 to 1860, they were the loveliest things afloat. Slipping easily through the belt of calms about the equator, beating reefed and close-hauled around the Horn, they were designed to show their best point of sailing in the trade winds, the steadiest and most dependable of the airs moving with the general circulation of the atmosphere.

These were the winds which enabled Columbus—untrained in celestial navigation, but a master of dead-reckoning—to return with extraordinary accuracy again and again to the Caribbean Islands of the New World. Originating a third of the way up and down the latitude of the earth, they blow diagonally down toward the equator across the oceans of the world. Their trend is westward, out of the northeast in the northern hemisphere, from the southeast in the southern and coming together in a belt of calms called the *doldrums* where an ill-found sailing craft might lie for days, a painted ship upon a painted ocean.

Warmed by the heat of the sun, made lighter by the water dissolving into it from the oceans, the atmosphere above the equator is being urged constantly upwards. In this ascent clouds soon form, from which descend the heavy rains of the tropics. Acquiring additional heat as its water vapor gives up its store of stolen energy, the air rises eagerly until at about ten miles above the surface of the earth it reaches the base of the stratosphere. Here held down by the layer of warmer gas above it, the rising column can now only move north or south.

Its natural destination from the warm equator is each icy pole at the top and bottom of the world. But by one of her best tricks nature permits it to move only a third of this distance. There blowing toward the east, it sinks down to the surface, to return again to the equator where it is once more warmed and lifted.

Man moving slowly about his earthbound affairs is totally unaware of this piece of legerdemain which is going on continually in the air he breathes. But a fast-flying airplane or the projectile from a big gun finds itself being thrust always to the right in the northern hemisphere, to the left in the southern.

An immediate and demonstrable application of this same force may be noted in the whirling spiral which is produced when the drain is opened in a washbasin or bathtub; the whirl of the descending water is clockwise in the northern hemisphere, counterclockwise below the equator. A similar but simpler situation exists as a record is spun on a phonograph's turntable. The rim is moving around at a good clip, but the center is simply rotating. A fly moving inward or out would feel a sideways force which on the earth's spherical surface is given the name of *coriolus*.

On the spinning earth a Hottentot on the equator travels thousands of miles through space between one sunrise and the next, while an Esquimo near the North Pole moves but a few hundred. This motion is unfelt by either man, but if the Esquimo moved south to the home of the Hottentot, he would have to acquire in his journey the latter's circular velocity.

The air moving away from the equator below the stratosphere is spinning as the earth spins eastward toward the rising sun. In its progress towards the poles, it must retain this easterly flow. But with each mile it moves north or south, the spherical earth is shrinking in girth and traveling a shorter distance each day. As the stars see it, it is the air that is attempting to blow in a straight line, while the earth is moving more slowly as the winds aloft flow toward the north or south.

But to a pilot, lifting his plane to fifteen or twenty thousand feet above Bermuda, the result will be a helping tail wind on the long flight to Lisbon or the Azores.

GENERAL CIRCULATION OF THE ATMOSPHERE

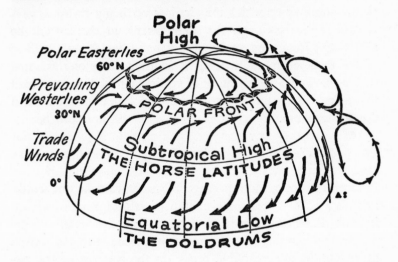

Around thirty degrees of latitude, this upper air is traveling almost due east. Here it meets other colder winds from the north or south; its journey from the equator is completed. Cooled by the air from higher latitudes, the tropic winds sink slowly towards the earth's surface, where they take up their return trip. Here they are faced with the same force of coriolus, but now the result is reversed. The bulging earth is moving a greater distance in each daily spin, as the winds move down along the surface returning to the equator. The air therefore lags more and more behind each new spot it reaches and comes to blow more and more towards the west as an east wind.

23

These are the steady, reliable trades. When at last they come together around the world's central belt, the sun's daily heat slows them down as it warms and lifts them. Although at some places about the equator their collision is violent, producing towering clouds and thunderstorms, more generally the air at the surface has little of the sideways motion that seamen know as wind. This is the doldrums, the base of a great atmospheric chimney up which the air rises vertically.

Here it receives anew the solar energy which drives it up and away. Returning again after it has traveled only a third of the distance to each pole, its journey completes the first cell in the world-wide pattern of vertical circulation, by which the air moves continually around our globe below the base of the stratosphere.

II

Over the long, slow passage of geologic time the earth, scientists believe, has come to spin more and more slowly on its axis. Pulled by the mass of the moon, the waters of the oceans rise and fall a few feet or inches twice each day, acting as an almost imperceptible brake on the rotation of the terrestrial top. If this theory is correct, the time from one sunrise to the next must have been shorter millions of years ago, than it is today.

When the earth spun faster, so too must have the heated air rising turbulently above the hot equator. The greater motion, carried north or south as this tropic air moved sideways at the top of the troposphere, would have turned these winds sooner to an easterly flow, so that their outward journey would to that extent have been shortened. Today there are three circuits that the atmosphere completes in each hemisphere. But as the earth first cooled, as the sea and land were formed and as at last life came to exist, the circulation of the atmosphere may have been entirely different then than we know it to be now.

The relation between climate and geology is curiously close; any basic change in the way the air may have moved about the earth would have imposed corresponding changes on the weather of any geologic era. For example, the record of the rocks shows that semitropical conditions once existed for a long time well into the Arctic Circle.

This warmth must have been supplied from some other, hotter part of the world. The air, gaining heat each day within the tropics, is always radiating away in the arctic regions the extra energy brought up to it by the moving atmosphere. As it is now, so it must have been from the beginning of time, the earth's shape having always curved here away from the shafts of incoming sunlight.

The air above the poles sinks, like a puddle of glue or molasses, slowly towards the ice and snow below it. For six months of the year, during the darkness of the polar night, practically no solar heat is received. During the long day of its summer neither pole obtains much warmth from the sun resting low on the horizon. The arctic air, therefore, cools steadily in its slow descent earthward, radiating away its energy into outer space.

At the surface the descending currents are further chilled by contact with the ice and snow or the even colder ground. Sluggishly at first they then move horizontally away from the top and bottom of the world. Faster and faster, as more sinking air crowds down on them, the surface winds blow towards the far distant equator. As their speed increases, they find the world below them spinning a greater and greater distance every twenty-four hours. Although like all moving matter they attempt to follow a straight path, they appear to us on earth to blow like the trade winds out of the east.

Compared to the steady, reliable trades, however, their pattern is much more unpredictable. The world's geography, the changing seasons and the irregular pulsings in the atmosphere's pressure cause them at times to break forth in great forays. At others they seem to sulk in their cold heart-land and allow the warmer winds from the tropics to blow up unopposed on great invasions of their melting sheets of frozen water.

Swaying back and forth above the sixtieth parallel of latitude there runs a meteorological front in this never-ending battle between the cold and warm winds. In this conflict the polar air is lifted to the base of the stratosphere. Here it flows back to north or south pole above which it again settles, to return in due course, cold and heavy, to the frozen surface of the earth.

III

A third of the way up from the equator, a third of the way down from each pole, lie the boundaries of the third cell in the vertical circulation of the atmosphere. Within this middle belt of the earth's latitudes are most of the developed resources, the material wealth and the civilized culture of modern man. In the early history of the human race, however, this region in Europe and Asia was a rough frontier country out of which descended recurring tides of savage, hardy barbarians.

The first civilized communities were founded far to the south, along the great rivers of Mesopotamia or on the Indus or the Nile. No doubt in the intervening thousands of years the local climate of India, Asia Minor and Egypt has changed considerably. Yet the fact remains that here the weather is primarily a calm and equitable thing, changing slowly and predictably with the seasons, about which so much of primitive religion seems to have been constructed.

26

The westward tide of empire that followed in historical times flowed northward as well. Here man moved into new lands where, superimposed on the regular heat of winter and summer, there is a rhythm in the weather much more syncopated and irregular than anything he had known to the south where he had built his first cities and states. The energy and drive of Western Man may well be in large part derived from his move into a new environment where the weather and the way it changes are entirely different from what they were in his original tropical Garden of Eden.

Of the three circuits in which the atmosphere circulates in each hemisphere, the most interesting and irregular is this one in the middle. Lying between the cold polar and the hot tropical, it acts as a balance wheel and safety valve to the other two, adjusting itself continually to the world-wide surges that animate the troposphere.

In both halves of the world the air in this center cell blows generally from west to east, faster than the moving earth. Like a boy whipping a spinning top, the force of this motion counteracts the polar easterlies and the trade winds. If such westerly wind did not somewhere blow across the earth, the surface currents in the other two cells, pushing against our turning planet, would act with the tides to reduce the speed of its spin and would probably by this time have stopped its rotation completely.

Moving generally from west to east, the air in this central cell moves at the same time north along the surface in our half of the world, back south aloft at the top of the troposphere. Here above the thirtieth parallel of latitude it meets and mixes with the upper winds blowing north from the equator. Together these currents cool and sink toward the surface. Over the oceans they form a belt of calms which seamen named the horse latitudes, probably because here they had so often to

27

throw overboard the horses that were making such inroads on their supplies of fresh water.

Over land the upper air descends stripped of the water vapor which it was forced to surrender as it rose originally to these high levels. Therefore the great deserts of the world, the Sahara and the Gobi, those in Arabia and in our own Southwest, are situated along the line where the dry air from the base of the stratosphere sinks earthward to resume its journey back to the equator or northward toward its eternal battle with the cold polar air.

The changing fortunes of this conflict account for the alterations, often rapid and sometimes extreme, which characterize the weather in our so-called temperate zone. Such fluctuations largely obscure the over-all pattern of the air's circulation in this middle cell. But in general our winds blow from the northwest in winter, out of the southwest during the summer, as they move here between two great atmospheric circuits, one rising turbulently above the equator, the other sinking slowly toward the cold pole.

IV

The origins of man are shrouded in mystery, hidden in time. All that the anthropologists, the scientists of this subject, have on which to base their findings are a few imperfect skulls, some teeth and a somewhat more extensive array of other human bones. Such evidences of man's earliest existence are widely scattered across the earth's surface. Appearing in Europe, Africa, Palestine, northern China and the East Indies, they suggest that men or their immediate anthropoidal ancestors had already spread all about the world.

By historical times, mankind seems to have arranged itself into several distinct races. Giving them their popular names, we find the Caucasian in Europe, the Semitic in Asia Minor, the Negroid in Africa and the Mongolian in eastern Asia. To the early students of ethnology, which is the science that deals with the races and families of men, the explanation of such a distribution of different peoples was that true man, Homo sapiens, had first wandered away from some original common Garden of Eden. And then in widely varying geographical environments, his descendants had slowly acquired the particular racial characteristics that we see today.

As increased ethnic evidence accumulated, however, it showed clearly that the races of mankind were not once so simply divided, each more or less to its own continent. The existing distribution had instead occurred in comparatively recent times, as successive tribes or peoples, expanding in population, had coalesced under able leadership and then burst out of their homeland, bent on expansion and conquest.

Long before the era of such profitable wars and excursions, man, organized in small tribal societies, seems to have been spread all about the earth. Here many such aboriginal peoples were in due course conquered by Scythian or Goth, Turk or Tartar, by Jap or Zulu, by Arab or Englishman. The existing pockets of such original tribes indicate pretty definitely that the races of mankind date back to a much earlier period in human history, and that they were then geographically distributed entirely differently than they are today.

Negroid characteristics, for example, are not confined to Africa. They are found half the world apart, on the Islands of Melanesia and along the shores of the Baltic. Western man, for a second case, may have come a longer way to reach Europe than he did to discover America, since the aboriginal Ainus of Japan and the Polynesian seafarers of the Pacific are more closely related to Europeans than they are to any of their nearer human neighbors.

All the evidence of anthropology and ethnology seems to agree on one point, that man from his earliest existence was a wanderer, a continual migrant out of choice or necessity. In his survival, in his quest for food, he lived first by his wits as an individual hunter and then by his ability to organize a tribal battue. The tribe moved, as the game moved. When the beasts diminished or disappeared, man either migrated or died.

In addition to the animals of field or forest, another prolific source of sustenance was the teaming life of the seashore. Along the north coast of Germany are great mounds of shells and other refuse left by the primitive peoples who camped there each summer, feasting on the sea's bounty. Although there is little tangible proof as to man's ability as a prehistoric fisherman, all existing primitive people who live by the ocean are astonishingly skilled at this ancient trade.

Offshore deep-sea fishing has been in modern times the usual breeding ground for seafaring. On land the geographical features of the earth's surface have largely determined the migrations of peoples. Originating generally in plain or steppe or other empty space, most conquering hordes have been channeled by mountain ranges through the great gaps or passes that lead into fertile lands beyond. The oceanic currents and the prevailing winds may well have acted in much the same way for any migrations that occurred upon the sea.

The evidence that such prehistoric maritime migrations did, in fact, take place is to some degree uncertain and in large measure indirect. A band of courageous Scandinavians recently set out to show how such a voyage could have been made across the Pacific. The account of their success is a modern classic of adventure, even though the proof of their thesis may well require additional support.

The explorations and conquests of earlier Norsemen occurred in historical times, floated by slim craft which primitive man might well have duplicated. The greatest known migration of this sort, however, occurred in the other principal ocean of the world. Although it was on a much more primitive basis than that of the Vikings, it was beautifully adjusted to the oceanic conditions with which it had to deal. Across hundreds of miles of the empty Pacific, an arc of islands from Australia to Hawaii was populated by the sea-loving Polynesians.

The records of these people, transmitted with great care albeit by word of mouth, recite not only the type of craft used and the seamanship employed, but also the marvelously simple methods of navigation by which their voyages between these pinpoints or handkerchiefs of land were repeated again and again.

Much more primitive voyages may well have been made, as *Kon-Tiki* suggests, on rafts, floated westward with the equatorial currents and pushed onward by a square sail spread to the easterly winds. Or, as another possibility, the summer sea route, favored by the Aleutian current and helped by the prevailing westerlies, seems in many respects an easier and more inviting means of moving from Asia into America than that across the Bering Sea and down along the rugged Alaskan coast.

Whether or not additional data will add weight to the theory that maritime migrations were an important method of distributing early man so widely about the world, the fact remains that in the growth of more modern empire, the winds that blow across the oceans were crucial. No reader of modern history can fully appreciate the development of commercial and military sea power without understanding the alternating belts of wind and calm that girdle the seas.

The doldrums which exist along the equator, the trade winds which blow to the north and south, the horse latitudes at about thirty degrees of north and south latitude, and the Roaring Forties above and below this second belt of calm airs, all these appear in stories and accounts of the sea. The existence and direction in which blow the prevailing winds deter-

31

mined the routes or courses of the merchant and battle fleets of all the nations, of successive captains, corsairs and merchant adventurers.

V

In the Middle Ages, relying on the authority of the Bible, man believed that the earth stood stationary at the center of his universe. The movement of the stars was explained by the rotation of the celestial sphere, these bright spots in the firmament being in some accounts the peepholes through which the angels looked down from heaven upon earth. Poetic as this explanation may seem, it presented no particular observable difficulty in the days before the invention of the telescope. But in the case of the planets—those wanderers through the heavens—a considerably more involved mechanism was needed to account for their eccentric paths across the sky above a motionless earth.

There is a story, variously told, about a Royal Prince of Castille who was having to learn about the complicated cycles and epicycles by which Ptolemy, the Alexandrine Greek, allowed for the planetary motions. This instruction was being given sometime in the thirteenth century, and one account states that young Alphonso expressed his royal surprise that God had not created the world to some better, simpler plan.

To the modern schoolboy the findings that brought Galileo before the Inquisition may still seem pretty involved. But the daily rotation of the earth and its annual swing around the sun are easy enough to visualize. The complication which causes his difficulty is the same one that produces the alternation of the seasons.

How the axis of the earth got tilted in the first place is something of a mystery. In the geologic history of the world, there is evidence that at first the world may have spun more nearly upright, at right angles to the orbit it traverses in twelve months about the sun. Perhaps the change came when and if a part of the earth was spun off, out of what is now the Pacific Ocean, to form the moon. Or possibly the great masses of ice that were built up within the arctic regions caused during these glacial periods a shifting of the line about which the earth spins. Or perhaps, like a wobbling top, the effect results simply from the slow decrease in the speed of the earth's rotation.

However it may have come about, this tilting of the poles is what causes the annual cycle of our climate, the seasons of the year. All the world's weather is affected by the sun's apparent march back and forth across the equator. Then, as the position of the sun at midday moves, the two halves into which the earth is divided geographically become unbalanced meteorologically.

During our northern winter, for example, the polar cell of circulation expands, its boundary moving steadily southward as the air grows slowly colder during the long arctic night. As our days grow longer, on the other hand, the warm air curculating in the tropical cell moves north, supplying additional reinforcements to beat back the stubbornly retreating forces from the Pole.

Thus with the seasons the system of circulation in one half of the world contracts, while the three cells in the other half expand. But these adjustments in the restlessly moving air cannot happen instantaneously. Time is required for the atmosphere to work out its changes. Directly below the source of heat, the air within the tropics quickly follows the solar march, the doldrums and the trade winds shifting easily with the sun. But to the north and south, the seasonal changes in the earth's weather lags more and more behind the calendar.

The temperate zone in which we live is covered by the intermediate cell which takes the brunt of these seasonal alternations. For a few weeks in late summer and winter the atmosphere has pretty well adjusted itself to the changes which the sun is imposing upon it. But for the rest of the year, our weather is constantly pulsating between the thrusts of the warm and active southern air moving readily with the sun's progress and the cold, heavy winds of the north stubbornly resisting the adjustments of the seasons.

The way in which the sun appears to move tends to intensify this conflict. Independently of the alternation of day and night, the sun at midday moves higher in the heavens during the spring and sinks lower again each day in autumn. The shape of this apparent motion in time is like that of a wave in space. Moving most slowly in June and December, it first establishes its crest and six months later its trough, when it has shifted some twenty-three and a half degrees away from the equator. In March or September, however, its noontime position is advancing or retreating north or south at its fastest rate, forming, as it were, the slopes of the wave.

To the man in the street these are the times of year when the days grow longer or shorter most quickly. But in the weather this is the season when the atmospheric cells within the tropics are shifting the fastest north and south, while within the arctic regions little or no seasonal change has as yet occurred. The resulting alterations in atmospheric flow are therefore at these times of year the most rapid and violent, so that spring and autumn are the seasons of the great storms which may sweep for several days across our middle latitudes or twist as terrible hurricanes within the tropics.

Tropical weather is largely controlled by the sun's annual progress. The rainy season is followed by the months when the sun shines steadily. To the dwellers in these regions therefore the sun naturally became a deity upon which their crops and their flocks depended. With prayer and ritual the early priests tracked or plotted its noontime position from magnificent pyramids or by primitive plinths. In simple superstition or with complicated mysteries its highest point was celebrated, as the green fields ripened into brown in midsummer, its lowest position bewailed for fear it should not ascend the skies again for the spring planting.

As civilization expanded and man moved northward out of his original homeland, he found a meteorological situation that was far less simple. Outside the tropical belt the vertical circulation of the atmosphere is modified by other forces which make our weather the shifting, uncertain thing it is. Here on the earth's surface are differences in geography to which the atmosphere is forced to adjust. Lifted by the great mountain ranges, heated over hot deserts, chilled by expanses of arctic snow and ice, the air moves erratically, reacting locally to such specialized conditions.

Yet the overriding geographic difference is that between land and water. Whereas the continents warm up quickly and cool off rapidly, the oceans are storehouses of the sun's heat, remaining at much the same temperature the year round. At the same time their moving waters distribute this stored heat to the colder parts of the world by great currents such as the Gulf Stream.

The three cells in each hemisphere are, to be sure, the basic pattern of the vertical circulation of the atmosphere. But the air is likewise turned into great circular whirlpools which move parallel to the earth's surface. These horizontal movements form a second meteorological design, which in its own way changes with the seasons and maintains its own rhythm, as the continents heat up more rapidly in summer and cool off more quickly in winter than do the oceans that surround them.

CHAPTER III

The Little Wheel Runs by Faith

I

TO the schoolboy the world is laid out as a rectangular map, on which Greenland is a large continent and the distance across the Atlantic is much the same at Boston as it is at Miami. The progress of learning, in this case as unfortunately in so many others, requires a prior step of unlearning. After being introduced to the work of the great Mercator, it is not always easy for us to form a proper picture of our global planet, to see the land and sea as on a sphere and in their true proportions. In a sense this is a pity, because there is indeed a curious relation between the continents and the oceans which cannot be envisaged from a flat projection.

About three quarters of the earth is covered by water. If this excess of sea is disregarded, we find that the northern hemisphere has ocean where the southern half has land, and vice versa. At the top of the world there is an Arctic Sea almost completely bounded by the northern shores of America, Europe and Asia, whereas the South Pole is centered on a continent entirely surrounded by water. The rest of the southern hemisphere is ocean except for Australia and two fingers of land, Africa and South America pointing down towards its pole. Conversely the great land masses of the world are situated in the northern half of our planet, with two narrowing oceans reaching upwards towards the Arctic Sea.

36

An imaginative eye—considering this relationship which is much like that of a photographic print to its negative—might well reach the conclusion that the continents of the world were originally designed to cover the surface of a much smaller planet, that the dry land, like a pair of pants on a fast-growing adolescent, has been split apart to cover a larger global expanse than was at first intended. There is an obvious neatness about the way the eastern shores of the new world seem to fit into the western edge of the old. Then, too, the islands connecting Australia with the Asiatic mainland look like a bent hinge about which this island continent has swung as it split away from the Indian peninsula.

There is quite a respectable mass of supporting data to reinforce the possibility of such continental drifting. The initial starting point of such a theory is that the moon was spun out of the earth at the time when its molten rock and liquid metal first began to cool and harden. The Pacific Ocean, with its incredible deeps, ringed by mountains and volcanoes, is the area from which the lunar mass is assumed to have come and toward which the continents of the rest of the world have been trying to move.

When this idea was first suggested, its action could only be imagined as having taken place aeons ago. The only possible assumption to be made was that the earth had acquired an initial store of heat at its creation, and that thereafter down the ages this supply of energy had been steadily dissipated. On a continuously cooling world, any movements of the continents must have been completed long ago, the volcanic eruptions and mighty earthquakes that are still experienced being merely the last vestiges of the titanic forces which rocked the world much earlier in geologic time.

Yet there were difficulties inherent in this otherwise clear position. The geologic age before our present one was an era of massive formations of snow and ice. But there are clear indications on the rocks of India, for example, that other periods of the same sort had occurred in earlier times. To account for such recurrences of cold and glaciation, some other explanation had to be found. By some scientists the burden of proof was shifted to the shoulders of the atmosphere. Changes in the nature of our gaseous blanket explained how extra amounts of heat from time to time were allowed to escape into outer space.

At the turn of the century a simpler explanation became possible. As a result of Becquerel's inadvertent discovery, the earth was seen to have within itself, bound up in the heart of certain of its atoms, a source of latent energy. This store, as it was studied by the Curies, is released as inexorably as fate, without relation to those factors, such as temperature or pressure, of chemical affinity or electrical difference, which trigger all the previously known ways of forcing nature to change her shape.

Uranium and thorium are reasonably abundant about the earth's surface. But although they are two of the heaviest elements, they are found only in the rocks of the earth's outer covering. Surprisingly enough they do not seem to be distributed deep within our planet's molten core, their chemistry accounting for their distribution. As a result the earth appears to possess in its solid crust a supply of heat which may well have produced the volcanic activity which time and again has dynamically ended each long era of geologic quiet.

The extreme cold of the ocean deep is evidence that little of the heat of the earth's internal fire is lost upwards. For long periods a dweller on the surface would have no sign of the forces building up within the interior. Solid as the earth may seem beneath his feet, man is living on a thin shell covering a ball of molten metal. For aeons of time, this interior furnace lies docile and quiet. When it has erupted intermittently down the ages, showing its inner power, the effect upon weather and climate, upon the delicate heat machine which maintains life in the world, has been equally violent.

Scientists do not know whether the world is now emerging from the final stage of the last Ice Age or whether we are living in an intermediate period after which the great ice sheets will return. Interestingly enough no great drop in the world's average temperature seems to be required to have produced the vast fields of ice which rose thousands of feet above northern Europe, Asia and America. Their great weight, pressing down on the surface of the earth, is one of the few known and measurable forces powerful enough to have produced the changes that geology records.

By relatively minor alterations in the geography of the world—in the height of its mountain ranges or the currents of its restless oceans—there could arise corresponding changes in the circulation of the atmosphere. The air, carrying its dust and water vapor, is the means by which the heat of the tropics is brought up to the poles, its movements in a large measure determining the climates of the world.

II

The breeding place of life, the Garden of Eden for the first living things, was originally the prehistoric sea. The saltiness of human blood may well indicate that our earliest animal ancestors took with them onto land their oceanic environment, our blood's temperature being that of the water from which they emerged. If this was so, this water was hot. Indeed the climate of the world for most of its history has been generally and consistently warmer than it is today.

In those earlier days the earth may have been closer to the sun. Or it may have been warmed by more of its original heat. But the earth itself may equally well have determined its own climate. During these periods of greater warmth, when temperate conditions reached up into the arctic, the continents were all lower than they are today, with large portions of them covered by swamps and shallow seas.

Land and water react quite differently to the sun's radiation, continents and oceans having as a result curiously contrasting climates. Rock and sand heat up quickly and cool off rapidly, so that a continental climate is marked by extremes of winter cold and summer heat.

Oceans and seas, on the other hand, are reservoirs of heat. More than twice as much of this energy is required to raise the temperature of water than is needed to heat the land an equal amount. In addition only the top skin of the solid earth is heated. At the beach in summer the scorching sand is cool just below the surface. But the sun's rays penetrate into the transparent water, where the restless waves then act to distribute it further within a depth of several hundred feet.

Storing up the large amounts of heat in summer which it draws on steadily during winter, the oceans enjoy a climate which is much milder and more equable than that over land. When the continents were low and generally wet and swampy, the world's climate would have been predominantly maritime rather than continental. With no great mountain ranges to interrupt the flow of the surface winds and no high land masses on which ice and snow could build up, the winds and waters of the world would have been better able to carry the warmth of the tropics north and south toward the poles.

Unlike the solid land, the gaseous air and the liquid ocean move dynamically under the impulsion of the sun's heat. Acting together they form gigantic whirlpools of movement each in its own element. In the seas these are the currents such as the Gulf Stream and the Japanese Current which sweep north in our hemisphere along the eastern edge of America or Asia and then return as cold streams down the western shores of Europe or the west coast of Canada and the United States.

In the air over the oceans a pattern of horizontal rotation is imposed on the vertical circulation of the atmosphere. Above the horse latitudes, close to the thirtieth parallel, the air sinks down dry and clear from below the base of the stratosphere. Here in the Atlantic and Pacific oceans the winds develop a circular sweep, forming two enormous wheels, one north, the other south of the equator in each ocean. Each pair moves as if geared together, the ones in the North Pacific and North Atlantic turning clockwise, the two in the opposite half of the world spinning in the contrary direction.

In their rotary sweep above the ocean currents the winds move outwards, as the vertical circulation of the atmosphere feeds new air down into their centers. These therefore are areas of high barometric pressure and generally fine, clear, sunny weather. The islands, such as Bermuda, the Azores and those of the Hawaiian chain which lie in this belt of weather, are famous as preferred playgrounds for the luckier members of mankind.

Further out nearer their edges, the air moves faster. A mass of such air will from time to time be spun off like mud from a spinning wheel. Up from the Caribbean such an air mass will bring warm weather to the eastern United States; down from the North Pacific another such will carry a storm of rain or snow into the northwestern states. Such air, dry and warm when it first starts outward, will be moist and wet by the time it reaches the outer fringes, its temperature depending upon the sector of the circle from which it breaks away.

The winds in the center of each ocean blow out of the east along the equator. In our hemisphere they then swing northward as they approach the land. At about the forty-fifth parallel of latitude they become enmeshed with two smaller atmospheric wheels which, at the top of the North Atlantic and Pacific oceans spin oppositely to those to their south.

Below Iceland and the chain of the Aleutian Islands the

41

warm moist air, moving up with the Gulf Stream or the Japanese Current, meets the cold winds from the arctic. As it approaches this collision, the southern air is carrying about all the moisture it can hold. At the first chilling contact with the winds from the polar regions, it is lifted aloft to form fog and thick, low-lying clouds. Out of these rain or snow falls as the rule rather than the exception.

The steady formation of fog and cloud in these particular areas acts like a gigantic mouth, sucking in the air which is bringing to it new supplies of invisible water vapor. Its collapse into water droplets or ice crystals supplies in turn the force of the suction. The action is thus largely self-perpetuating. As a result, the barometric pressure is here characteristically depressed, and these two smaller atmospheric wheels are called the Icelandic and Aleutian lows.

The center of the larger circuits to their south are known as the North Pacific and the Bermuda highs. Above the North Pole another area of high pressure exists where the air sinks slowly downward, in accordance with the atmosphere's general trend of vertical circulation. As the cold northern winds then move southward across the spinning earth, they come to blow out of the northeast as the polar easterlies. Thus around the top of the world a third and final atmospheric wheel spins oppositely to those centered above Iceland and the Aleutians.

A similar center of high pressure exists over the continent of Antarctica, but here there are no land masses to channel the air into corresponding areas of bad weather. Instead, all around the southern ocean there is a practically continuous belt of low pressure along the sixtieth parallel of south latitude. Except for a few ships of exploration or an occasional whaler, only a few vessels seeking passage around South America now enter these inhospitable waters. But before the building of the Panama Canal in the old days of sail, the weather here was a symbol of about the worst meteorological conditions to be encountered anywhere on the surface of the sea.

III

The great crinkles in the earth's crust that we know as mountains are evidence of the titanic forces by which the world has from time to time been tortured. Puzzling as their formation may be to the geologist, their meteorological action is observably clear and direct. They are one of the most important factors in determining climate.

Where they face the prevailing winds, the air is forced to rise rapidly to the condensation level, there to shed its moisture as rain or snow. Their windward slopes, therefore, as in our northwest, are covered with heavy vegetation; jungles in the tropics, forest in the temperate zones. On their lee side the air descends stripped of its water vapor and warmed by the heat given up as the clouds were formed on the opposite slopes. Here then is an area of general aridity. The mountains of eastern Australia make the center of this subcontinent largely an arid desert. The Andes have the same effect upon northern Chile.

The great chains that run north and south receive in this way the prevailing winds which blow predominantly with or against the spinning earth. Those that run east and west act somewhat differently. The greatest of these controls the activities of more than half the human beings living on the earth. Starting from the west in Turkey, it runs eastward through Persia into Afghanistan. Here it splits into a tilted V. One leg thrusts northeastward above Mongolia to the Bering Sea. The other points across the top of India, forming the Himalayas which include the highest mountains in the world.

The Alps, the Pyrenees and the Urals are only minor wrinkles on the earth's surface compared to these gigantic peaks

43

and plateaus. Except for the inverted triangle of India, they ring the southern and eastern borders of the greatest land mass on earth. The combined continents of Europe and Asia completely dwarf the size of Africa, America or Australia. Here in contrast to the even climate of the great oceans is exhibited the extremes of heat and cold, the seasonal changes in wind and weather that meteorologists mean by their term *continental.*

In the wastelands of northern Siberia is situated the *cold pole* of the world where the temperature in winter drops to its lowest known reading. Two thousand miles directly to the south lies the Gobi Desert where the heat in summer is about the same as on the equator. These, to man, are all empty, barren lands. But below them in India and China, among the wet fields and jungles of Burma, Siam and Malaya, live half the population of the world. Their whole economy, indeed their daily lives, depends in large measure on the successful operation of a climatic heat machine.

During the summer from the oceans that ring the south and east of Asia, moist air blows inland, up the slopes that lift toward the central mountains and tablelands. These bring the rains that are needed to water the crops on which this vast population subsists. When the sun turns south again in autumn, there is a meteorological pause while the lands to the north lose their heat. Then as the cold moves down from the arctic across the Siberian plain the winds begin to blow again, but now in the reverse direction, dry and comparatively cool, out of the north down the hills and mountains. With the spring there is a second period of calm, before the cycle is again resumed in summer.

Living generally at the bare level of subsistence, this concentration of human beings exists as if keeping time to the rhythm of these seasonal winds. If the beat ever syncopates, coming down a little early or a bit late, if it is struck too lightly

or heavily, disaster will overtake some part of this over-
populated land. For example, when warm winds in spring
bring too much rain to the headwaters of the great Chinese
rivers, the Yangtse or Hang-Ho will flood the low-lying lands
along its shore, destroying the homes and crops of millions.
Or perhaps over some province of India low-flying clouds in
summer sweep north, refusing to give up enough of their life-
giving rain, until the drying earth is parched and starvation
stalks the impoverished villages.

The *monsoons,* as these seasonal winds are called, dominate
all of central Asia and the seas and islands that ring a third
of its borders. From western China to the mountains guarding
northwest India the high land lies like a bowl, within which
the summer temperature rises steadily as the sun's heat warms
the earth below it. When in time this heated air starts rising,
enough atmospheric suction must first be built up, like a fire
in a poor chimney, to pull the air lying over India and its
ocean, over China and its seas, up the slopes of the encircling
chain of mountains. When at last the monsoon winds start to
blow, their effect is felt as far away as Ceylon, Borneo or the
Philippines, over an arc of thousands of miles of island and
ocean.

In winter the same mountains act for a while as a barrier
to the cold air moving down from the north. When in due
course Siberia has become as cold as the North Pole, it becomes the center for its own column of heavy descending air.
When this chill current then surmounts the obstacle of the
surrounding mountain chain, the air pours out of its cold
homeland much like the floods that follow the breaking of a
real dam. On a smaller scale similar conditions exist over the
plateau of Greenland and probably account for the force of
the winds blowing out of the high lands of Antarctica.

The continental climate of Asia is the most extreme example of the way in which a large land mass can change, summer

and winter, the nature of the atmosphere lying over it. In July and August it is an area of low barometric pressure, where the air, after shedding its moisture on the slopes of the rim, rises above the dry, hot bowl of the Asiatic desert. In January and February, on the other hand, a center of atmospheric high pressure settles over Siberia, while the air, heavy and cold, seeks an outlet across the mountains into the hot lands and the more distant seas to the south and southeast.

On a smaller scale the same seasonal cycle operates in all the continents of the world, wherever a land mass in summer warms up sufficiently the air lying over it and chills it off correspondingly in winter. But without some range of high mountains to squeeze out the incoming water vapor from the oceans, this process is comparatively mild and gentle. Alaska without the northern Rockies would probably enjoy a climate not much worse than England's. When the earth lay low beneath the sweep of the ocean's winds, the heat of the tropics could circulate much more easily into the Far North and the climate of the world would have been considerably more salubrious.

IV

Storms and bad weather are formed out of conflict, such struggles occurring as a result of atmospheric differences. In meteorology, as in human affairs, its examination is dramatic. But in the history books battle, conquest and personal combat are perhaps recounted at too great length; too much space is probably accorded the heroes and the generals. The accommodation of disputes or the arrangement of disagreements makes, it is true, less interesting reading, but this pacific process is surely of vastly more importance in the progress of the race.

The writers of American history, in this view, are at fault in giving so much space to the campaigns of the Civil War and in not recounting more fully the policies of vindictiveness and repression which rubbed such hateful salt into the wounds of strife. For here was one of the great object lessons on how to win a war and destroy a peace, complete with an apostle preaching the wiser course to follow, removed by the hand of a small-minded neurotic at the exact moment when Lincoln's real task was about to begin.

The science of meteorology cannot, for its part, fully recount the story of the shifts in pressure, of the pulsings and throbbings that move the weather to its changes and its conflicts. A reading of history suggests that there have been similar inexplicable urges in the human race. For example, the great migrations of Mongol, Vandal and Goth seem clearly to have been something more than barbaric tribes looking simply for greener pastures or richer towns to loot.

Some deeper explanation is certainly needed for the explosive energy and untaught ability of Genghis Khan and his lieutenants, or for the strange drive that carried a substantial segment of the Gothic tribes across France and Spain, to disappear into the rugged, inhospitable mountains of northwest Africa. In the Middle Ages, when no means of rapid communication existed, the spread of the Children's Crusade and the outbreak of the Peasants' Revolt are two typical cases in point. Both seem to have arisen from impulsions which were apparently felt by astonishing numbers of people over wide stretches of country.

Perhaps civilization has educated some sixth sense out of us which man originally inherited from his animal ancestors. Be that as it may, there is much that is still to be discovered about the weather. Yet the clearest and most understandable cause of its changes is the progress of the seasons. Although the climate of North America is less affected than that of the vast continent of Eurasia, here in summer the hot and lifting air welcomes the wet winds from our adjacent oceans, while in winter the cold air of the north drives heavy and powerful down the central plains to the Gulf of Mexico.

During the long cycle of the arctic night, the single cell of high pressure above the North Pole splits in two, one centered over Siberia, the other taking station above upper Canada. Between these two, at the heads of the oceans, the Aleutian and Icelandic lows are at this time of year expanding the area of their vile weather to its fullest extent.

To the south the air of the tropics sinks downward above the horse latitudes. Over the North Atlantic little circular motion of the air remains with winter in possession of Europe and of our continent. Instead the trade winds blow firm and strong out of the northeast. The vastly larger Pacific, however, retains its center of high pressure, which, considerably shrunken in extent, lies above the Hawaiian Islands.

From the equator up to the middle latitudes the atmosphere in January and February circulates primarily according to its main vertical pattern. Along the Arctic Circle, on the other hand, four cogged atmospheric wheels spin principally horizontally. Within the two on land the air is descending and moving sluggishly outward, while in the two at the tops of the oceans, it works slowly inward and back up towards the stratosphere.

As the days lengthen into spring, the temperatures of land and sea come back into balance. The arctic high returns to its position over the pole, while the Aleutian and Icelandic lows grow smaller and less vigorous. Over the oceans, the air assumes a rotary motion as the areas of high pressure expand over the North Pacific and between Bermuda and the Azores.

With July the continents grow hot, welcoming in the maritime air spun off the oceans' expanding atmospheric whirlpools. In Asia the monsoons start to blow strongly against the mountains, while in our continent warm, muggy winds sweep out of the Gulf up the Mississippi, bringing us a heat wave which in August may reach up to the shores of Hudson Bay.

Thus in summer the relation between the air's horizontal and vertical circulation is reversed. In the middle latitudes the movement is predominantly rotary, its descent centered over the oceans, its lifting occurring over the hot land. Within the Arctic Circle, on the other hand, the air sinks down slowly above the pole, moving out of the northeast against the warm southern winds. To sweep down and end a summer session of the heat and high humidity coming to us from the oceans, some extra force of pressure is required high above the pole where the air is sinking down from the top of the troposphere.

CHAPTER IV

Say Not the Struggle Naught Availeth

I

ALL over the world men measure the wind and the temperature, the humidity and the barometric pressure, recording and reporting all the factors that determine the progress of the weather. In most civilized countries these stations are closely spaced, but at sea such observations are obtainable only from those relatively few spots where ships steam across the empty ocean.

Most weather arises through the conflict of maritime air with that which is bred over the continents. In forecasting such struggles the weather man is severely handicapped by his lack of a good reporting network across the seven seas. In this respect the change from sail to steam was a backward step for the science of meteorology, despite its usefulness to the world's system of transportation.

The steamer lanes of today are much like well-traveled highways. Coming together at various geographic bottlenecks or maritime obstructions, such as the Panama Canal, the Straits of Gibraltar or the Cape of Good Hope, they fan out somewhat, but only a little, across the centers of the seas. An insignificant percentage of the ocean's weather is observed as a result.

Sailing ships, on the other hand, had to seek the best slant of wind, so that an outbound voyage often followed a totally

50

different course from that taken on the one inward-bound. Using mainly the steady trade winds, some American ships, trading to China during early Federal days, followed the practice of circling westward round the world.

The modern vessel, powered by steam or diesel engine, ploughs unromantically direct, following as closely as possible the appropriate great circle from landfall to landfall. A modern meteorologist may well look back with longing to the old days of sail, when in addition to the cargo and passenger craft, hundreds of clumsy whalers thrashed and wallowed about all the oceans of the world. If he could have them back, equipped with today's radio, the maps on which he plots the daily development of the weather would be much more accurate and complete where they cover the world's waters.

A satisfactory current substitute is provided by the weather ships sent out by the nations whose commercial aircraft fly the North Atlantic. Patrolling to the north of the European steamer track, the United States contingent is manned by the Coast Guard who have kept track, ever since the sinking of the Titanic, of the icebergs coming south with the Labrador Current.

These only constitute a danger to mariners during the summer when the glaciers of Greenland are melting, but now all the year round our cutters keep station, their weather reports comprising an essential part of the information by which the route and altitude of each transatlantic flight is planned.

Year by year new aircraft fly higher and higher, at levels where the thinning air permits greater and greater speed. The latest step in this trend is the commercial use of the jet engine, which can only operate efficiently or economically above fifteen thousand feet. As compared to the surface winds, the air at these altitudes moves in swift currents whose rhythms are related only on the broadest scale to the changes in the sea-

51

sons, to the differences between land and water, between high mountain and low river valley.

Before the last war the upper air was probed by complicated and expensive apparatus carried upwards by free balloons. Such radio-sounding devices are being now more and more supplemented by airplanes especially designed and fitted to investigate the wind and weather high aloft. From this data there is opening a new and fascinating chapter in meteorology. Here many of the forces which steer and guide the weather close to the surface seem to arise—forces which encourage the growth of its storms or restrain their urge to power.

This new chapter may well prove as exciting and valuable as the one that was formulated by Bjerknes in Scandinavia as the first world war was reaching a climax thirty-five years ago. In Norway at that time a novel theory was being advanced as to the formation of weather in our middle latitudes. Essential as Bjerknes' reasoning has become to the meteorologist and his science, the idea of contrasting masses of air and the concept of conflict between winds at different temperatures carrying varying amounts of moisture offer an explanation easily comprehensible to the man in the street. For him this theory has for the first time succeeded in making the weather and its development interesting and intelligible.

II

Shifting with the seasons, a meteorological battleline sways back and forth across the sixtieth parallel of latitude. This is the zone within which warm air out of the southwest meets the cold northeasterly winds blowing down from the arctic. By analogy with a military battle, it is called the *polar front*. Along it much of the weather of our middle latitudes is generated.

A front in the first world war was the line where the opposing systems of trenches faced each other across no man's
land. With the development of aviation in the last war, the
conflict was carried skyward. Depending on which side obtained supremacy in the air, the front aloft ranged forward
or far back of where the infantry was slogging it out on the
ground.

In much the same sense the contact between the contending forces of northern and southern air reaches thousands of
feet into the atmosphere. Stretching out along a gigantic curving surface, the polar front slopes upwards miles ahead of the
line where the two sets of winds are in contact close above
the ground.

In this meteorological conflict between north and south,
each army has its own tactics and strategy, each mass of air
has its own characteristic method of imposing victory or conducting a retreat. These maneuvers for the most part are
clearly observable in the changing weather, clarifying and
dramatizing its behavior for all who choose to recognize the
nature of this atmospheric struggle.

The difference between wet and dry air is observed daily in
human comfort, the contrast between cold and hot winds is
felt winter or summer as they blow against our cheeks. But
when two great masses of air, one warm and moist, the other
cold and dry, meet in collision, it is not easy for the average
person to visualize how differently they behave.

The best analogy may be drawn with molasses, glue or
heavy lubricating oil. When cold, such liquids are stiff and
sticky; when warm, they flow easily out of their containers.
To this picture, however, must be added the effect of the
water vapor in the warm air. As such air is lifted to the level
where its moisture begins to condense into cloud, it receives
additional warmth and lightness from the heat that is given
up in this process of thermal restitution.

When the warm winds blowing up from the southwest meet the cold air coming down from the opposite direction, they do not intermingle or mix. Instead each maintains its own individuality. The light southern air is lifted by the cold, much as water in a stream flows over a rocky ledge. To the heavy cold winds, hugging the ground, the warm air above them acts much like a gigantic tent, below which they are confined. Shaping itself into something like an enormous sloping mountain range the northern air presses a rounded shoulder of cold against the lighter air from the south.

With their line of contact stationary on the surface of the earth, the winds from the northeast and out of the southwest will be deflected from their original course, the arctic winds toward the west, the tropical air toward the east. Such a stationary front will then consist of two currents of air blowing past each other in approximately opposite directions, with a sharp change in temperature marking the transition from one mass of air to the other.

High above the earth, however, the lighter southern winds will still be flowing up and away northeastward, pressing as well as they can down against the sharply curving slope of the heavy air from the north. Wet as well as warm, these ascending airs form cloud as they pass through the condensation level. And this return of heat in turn urges them onwards and upwards.

Streaming away northward, the forces of the south must receive constant reinforcements simply to hold in check the more ponderous mass out of the north. When, with a winter's thaw or a summer heat wave, such reserves flow into the area of battle, the warm air is able to press down its opponent's curving outline into a long, flat, atmospheric ramp. At the foot of this the cold air retreats stubbornly along the surface of the earth.

When the southern winds are thus moving victoriously forward, the result is called a *warm front*. Its approach is noted by a steady thickening and lowering first of the high clouds and then of those in the middle levels. These indicate the position of the front aloft, where high overhead the warm air's moisture is condensing slowly and steadily. As the clouds come lower, rain will being to fall, the slow gentle rain best suited to refresh the ground after a period of long drought.

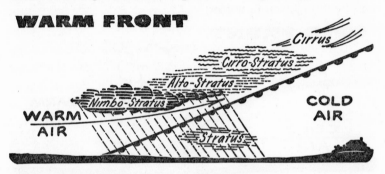

All during this time the cold air remains in possession of the lower layers. If it is sufficiently chill, as it sometimes is in winter, the rain will freeze to ice on trees and bushes and power lines. These destructive storms are the result of such hairline conditions that they are almost impossible to forecast accurately. Fortunately the temperature usually rises as the warm front moves closer along the surface. Then as the low clouds shred away, the sun comes out to melt the shining ice usually before it has built up sufficiently to cause much damage.

In summer when the forces of the south are strongest, the passage of a warm front brings us a spell of hot and humid weather. In winter, however, it is the northern air which generally has the upper hand. As it moves forward to the attack its rounded shoulder becomes more bulging. Supported by the strong frigid winds blowing down behind it, such a *cold front* lifts the lighter southern air rapidly and violently upwards.

55

A warm front may have the foot of its long atmospheric ramp in Virginia, while far to the north thickening clouds will be forming and the first light rain falling over New York and New Jersey. It heralds its approach by these atmospheric signals well in advance of its arrival on the surface. A cold front, on the other hand, strikes quickly and often without much prior warning. Towering clouds form along its edge, out of which if the opposing air is wet enough can come thunder and lightning even in winter.

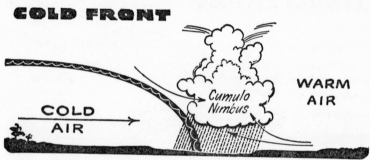

In contrast to the steady rain of warm front, the precipitation from a cold front will often be quick and violent, consisting of large drops like those from a summer thunderstorm. The winds, instead of being steady, are gusty and tempestuous, sometimes forming a long continuous line of the severe squalls which are so dangerous to the aviator or yachtsman. Whereas the clouds and rain associated with a warm front may hang around for hours, a cold front will usually move by in a matter of minutes, the quick drop in temperature, the sudden clearing and a sharp shift in the wind round to the northward evidencing the quick paroxysm of its meteorological intensity.

III

The victories and defeats, the advances and retreats observable in warm or cold front occur because the air over some

portion of the globe attains an individuality which it is then
unable or reluctant to surrender. Impelled by the mysterious
pulsings in the atmosphere, a great mass or puddle of air will
first break away from its original homeland. Where it then
meets air of different characteristics, a battleline is drawn,
running from the earth's surface thousands of feet skyward.

Such frontal zones are named according to the side which
is winning: warm if the southern forces are advancing, cold
if the northern air has the upper hand, stationary if a stalemate is in existence. These names catalogue, but cannot describe, the nature of each struggle. Sometimes the battle is
lightly contested; at others the fight may be long and stubborn.
In some cases one side may be overpoweringly strong; in
others the two forces more equally matched. As a result, the
passage of a front may be hardly noticeable or it may be a
thing of violence and destruction.

The degree of difference in temperature and humidity accounts for this wide range in frontal behavior. Hot and cold,
wet and dry, are not only the adjectives which describe the
properties of air masses, but they are likewise the essential
characteristics which in contrast determine the intensity of
the contest. The great contribution of Bjerknes and his fol-
lowers was first to assert this fact and then to show how each
mass of air attains its personality in the breeding ground that
is its region of origin.

Meteorology as yet cannot fully follow the shifting pressures
which move with the seasons through the horizontal and vertical circulation of the atmosphere. In periods of calm and
balance, the air rests quietly for days or weeks at a time over
hot desert, warm sea or frozen ice field. Here it acquires the
properties, in its temperature and humidity, which will enable
the weather men to give it a set of appropriate initials and to
anticipate much of its future behavior when in due course
it starts to move elsewhere.

Pushed outward by some extra weight in the upper atmosphere, spinning too fast at the outer edge of one of the great whirlpools of high or low pressure, a mass of air will leave its original source-region. Depending on where it was bred, the meteorologist tracking its course will write it as either *maritime* or *continental*, essentially as either wet or dry. As a measure of its temperature, he will further describe it according to the part of the world from which it comes, as either *equatorial, tropical, polar* or *arctic*.

Here the terms tropical and polar may be a trifle confusing. Tropical describes air that has its source along either of the tropics of Cancer or Capricorn, which mark the highest point up the earth's latitudes where the sun can be seen standing directly overhead at noon. Polar refers to an air mass bred above the polar front and does not relate directly to the poles themselves.

Due to the waist to which the American continent shrinks, little or no tropical continental air originates in Mexico to the south and enters the United States. Most of our warm southern air comes to us from the western edge of the North Atlantic high. From it moist, tropical maritime air flows into the eastern states or out of the Gulf of Mexico up the Mississippi Valley.

Such air moves north most vigorously in summer, when the hot land sucks and welcomes it in. In winter and early spring, on the other hand, polar maritime air, off the top of the Icelandic low, befogs the Grand Banks and eastern Canada, occasionally sweeping out of the northeast upon New England.

Out at sea below southern California, the winds of the North Pacific high are moving westward toward the distant coast of Asia. Where in their great circuit they return to meet the air moving back eastward below the Aleutian low, we have the source region for most of the weather that occurs along our northwestern seaboard. Such polar maritime air promptly sheds its moisture as rain or snow along the mountains of the coast and the vast chain of the Rockies further inland, the constant precipitation producing the fastest growing forests in this continent. Heated as its water vapor is wrung out of it, this air then descends into the central plains warm and dry. On our weather maps such air presents something of an anomaly. Cold and wet when it leaves its breeding ground below the Bering Sea, it eventually changes into the exact reverse after its passage of the mountains.

Lurking along the flank of the air moving in from the Pacific are the winds blowing down across the great shield of Canada. When this polar continental air, or its even colder cousin from the arctic, sweeps down in force out of the north, the maritime air from either ocean is pushed aside. In summer such an advance will end an August heat wave. In winter it will carry freezing temperatures into Texas or Florida. But all the year round these different air masses struggle for occupation of the air space over the United States, in their recurring battles bringing us the cycles that are characteristic of our changing weather.

In some other parts of the world, however, the meteorological picture is much simpler. Far to the south of us, where the bulge of Brazil thrusts out into the Atlantic, the climate is dominated by equatorial maritime air. Hot and moist it flows westward off the ocean, the astonishing amount of water vapor which it carries with it feeding the Amazon and its tributaries to form the largest river system in the world. When at last this air reaches the Andes, it swings south to meet continental tropical air moving up from the pampas of the Argentine.

A greater source of such hot, moisture-laden air is the vast Pacific Ocean. Punctuated only by an occasional island, the equator here runs nearly half around the world. In summer when the monsoon winds are blowing into central Asia, such equatorial air supplies its rain to the tremendous rim of lands stretching from India to Korea. When in winter the seasonal winds reverse their flow, the air from the central Pacific is deflected into the Indian Ocean, part of it curling back to blow against western Australia.

In the central desert of this subcontinent it meets tropical continental air. Replenished as it is from descending currents high in the atmosphere, such air is naturally dry, its source regions naturally arid. In the southern hemisphere, in South Africa and South America as well as Australia, it is tempered by the predominant maritime winds. But in North Africa and Asia few moisture-bearing breezes come in to counteract its dryness. So, as mentioned earlier, the greatest deserts of the world, the Sahara, the Arabian and the Gobi, here have their location and are the breeding grounds for the hottest, driest air to be found anywhere on earth.

IV

A storm tearing at the treetops, the rain beating against a window, a blizzard blanketing the countryside, each of these examples of the weather's power developed out of an initial state of calm. Somewhere this active air lay quiet and still, radiating away its heat over some dark, frozen land, or sopping up a store of water vapor from some warm sea.

The shifting pressure of the atmosphere discharges from time to time a mass of such air from its parent whirlpool. Like an army with banners it then issues from its original homeland and goes forth to conquer. Out of the major atmospheric collisions which then may follow can come in our latitudes the climax of wind, rain and storm.

In the pattern of the weather there is unfortunately no standard design. The generation of our storms, which the weather man resoundingly calls *extratropical cyclones,* generally begins with some slight kink or bend along a stationary front. The development at this stage is one of the trickiest problems for the forecaster. Sometimes such a shallow S-shape or wave, as it is termed, will straighten out again; at others it will rapidly grow deeper and more pronounced. Once firmly started, it is hard to stop; it is almost certain to expand both in power and in area.

Somewhere west of the Great Lakes, it may be assumed as a starting point, the polar front is lying stationary parallel to the Canadian border. To the eastward warm air moves up the Mississippi Valley, while to the west a thrust of cold winds is advancing southward out of upper Canada. On the right, therefore, the southern forces begin a slow advance as a warm front; to the left, the cold winds start pushing south as a cold front.

As the two attached fronts bend themselves into the deepening wave of such a horizontal S, clouds begin to form where the warm air is being lifted gently up the ramp of the warm front, more violently ahead of the bulge of the advancing cold front. A void or partial vacuum is thus created, as the gaseous water vapor collapses into its surprisingly more compact state of liquid water droplet or solid ice crystal. If now rain or snow starts to fall, carrying this solid or liquid water away earthward, the storm will, at least for a time, continue to expand.

A drop in the household barometer measures the decrease in atmospheric pressure that results from this process. Reacting to the suction, the air turns inward, beginning to flow around in the commencement of a great circular sweep. As the precipitation begins and new clouds appear, more and more air feels the impulsion to swing to its left toward the center of steadily decreasing pressure.

The light and volatile southern air reacts to this force more easily and readily than do the heavier, ground-hugging winds

61

THE DEVELOPMENT OF A
CYCLONIC STORM
SEEN FROM ABOVE

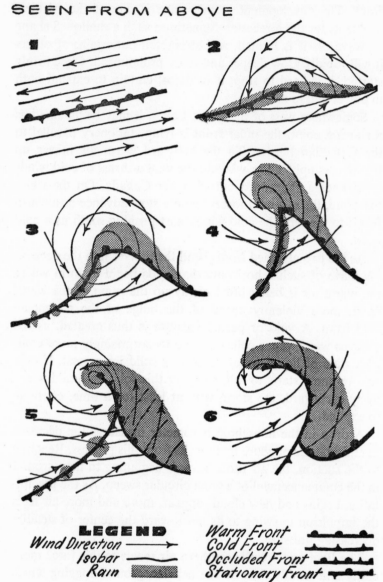

from the north. Expending much of its energy in supplying fresh water vapor to the storm's interior structure, the warm front creeps slowly forward, moving more slowly than the cold front advancing away to its left. As a result, the original symmetry between the two frontal systems disappears. Their shape begins to change from a flat S into a tilted V, its point at the center of the storm's circular spread.

As a whole this gigantic apparatus of growing cloud, whirling winds and falling rain moves eastward. As long as it receives additional supplies of water vapor from the air flowing into it, its power and extent will expand. As it crosses the Alleghenies or the last of the Great Lakes, such reinforcements are likely to come naturally into it. Here in its crescendo it begins to draw upon the moist air lying over the Atlantic.

As the rain or snow comes down across a parcel of northeastern states, the cold front in the meantime has been sweeping south in a great bulge across the Mississippi Valley. When this mass of air left its northern homeland, it took with it some of the characteristic rotation of an area of high atmospheric pressure. This is the opposite of the clockwise whirl of all storms in our hemisphere. Along its eastern edge, therefore, the cold winds are blowing most directly down from the north. On this side of their advance they assert their strongest power, a force which they will eventually surrender as they sweep south and west across the warmer land.

As the chill winds out of the northwest curl toward their right, they drive their cold front east and south. Moving strongly in behind the storm to the northeast, the front somewhere over Texas or the Southwest will come at last to a halt, its air no longer cold and powerful, blowing here gently, if at all, out of the east. When the old cold front thus becomes stationary, warm air off the Gulf or from over the Rockies may thrust against it. A new kink or wave may develop. The endless sequence of fair and foul weather may be about to start again in this corner of the country, while far away to the northeastward the old storm blows out to sea.

V

The air moving across the spinning earth is always urged towards its right in our hemisphere, towards its left in the other half of the world. This force, which increases with any object's speed, is greatest at the poles, falling off to nothing at the equator. In tropical hurricane and extratropical cyclone the air is forced to turn in the opposite direction, in the way it does not want to go, by the suction exerted at each storm's center.

This suction comes from an area of lowered atmospheric pressure created as water vapor condenses into cloud. Tropical hurricanes arise over the oceans, where supplies of such moisture-laden air lie all around the storm's periphery, ready to swirl in from all directions toward its central core. But in the middle latitudes the supply of moist air moves in from only one sector, where it is lifted and chilled by colder winds blowing in from a different side.

A tropical hurricane is a symmetrical vortex or whirlpool of wind and rain, while the storms that form outside the tropics—hence the term, extratropical—are marked by the discontinuities of cold and warm front. As such a storm, sweeping across the United States, approaches its maximum intensity, the long ramp up which the warm air is rising has been accordingly twisted from a flat slope into a spiral incline, swinging around a fair half of the storm's circumference.

Chilled in its lower levels by the colder air below it, this sector to the east and north is where the winds are strongest and most of the rain is falling. Across the rest of the circle, to the west and south, the cold front has swept forward and is about to overtake a portion of the warm front. As it does so, a third type of front comes into existence.

While the wind grows stronger and the area of cloud and rain expands, the cold front has been moving faster and more powerfully than the warm. In the illustration the two fronts where they rest on the surface form an inverted V, the warm front running diagonally northwestward out of the east, the cold front up from the southwest curving toward the north.

At the point of this V, part of the north winds now fall upon the exposed flank of the more slowly moving southern air. As the cold front's bulging edge lifts these weaker, warmer winds, it finds below them its own cousins from the north, air that may have been originally part of its own air mass. Yet no two parcels of air are ever exactly alike, all are conditioned and modified by the particular land or water over which they have traveled.

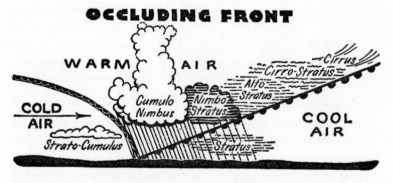

As such a storm approaches the eastern seaboard of our United States, the air in its northeastern sector is drawn more and more from the North Atlantic. Here then occurs a new conflict, of two currents of air both bred north of the polar front, but the winds behind the cold front originating in northern Canada, those below the warm front coming down perhaps from the Grand Banks. Thus as the cold front catches

65

up with the warm front and lifts it aloft, three masses of air, each with its own properties and special direction of flow, come into direct contact.

On the surface, blowing out of the east, is cold wet air, while pressing down above it moving north and west is the warm moist current from the south. Out of the north and west, pushing both of these other two out of its path, are the cold dry winds of the north. The formation of such an *occluded front* is part of the final paroxysm into which the storm is now developing.

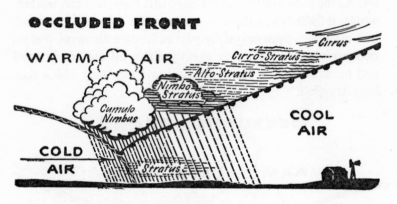

OCCLUDED FRONT

To the dentist an occlusion is how his patient's upper and lower teeth close and meet. Where the cold front has over-taken and begins to lift the warm front, the frontal system on the surface of the earth changes its shape from a tilted V to that of a lazy, inverted Y. Its tail, representing the occluded front, trails away north and west, the two arms indicating where warm and cold front still have their separate existence.

As this new sort of front grows longer, the cold advancing shoulder of the northern forces starts to shut off the flow of warm, wet, southern air into the center of the storm. These winds are thereupon deflected back toward their original breeding ground beyond Bermuda. With its supply of new moisture diminishing, the circling winds begin to fill up the central area of low pressure faster than its suction can be renewed by formation of cloud and rain. The occluded front becomes the dominant feature of the subsiding storm, as it moves finally westward out to sea.

Here the ocean and its warm Gulf Stream will iron out its last remaining atmospheric differences, those contrasts which in the first place caused this long climactic struggle. Swept along by the western winds, the fading storm will become a mere crinkle on the polar front across the north Atlantic. Meanwhile the currents of air which have been swept aloft throughout its whirling existence are perhaps giving some new nudge of pressure to the circulation of atmosphere, to produce somewhere else across the earth's surface a new outpouring of air from some other distant source-region.

CHAPTER V

Watching the Clouds Go By

I

GEOLOGISTS cannot agree as to whether the continents have drifted to their present positions or whether
they are situated now much where they have always been.
But the records of the rocks clearly indicate two things in
this respect. In the first place, the world from its earliest
beginnings seems to have been divided, as the Bible states,
into firmament and deep water. And secondly, the major
land masses of today appear to have been land ever since the
planet's molten sheath cooled to hardness.

Today the continents stand high above the levels of the
oceans. Throughout most of geologic time, however, this has
not been the case. Low-lying, swampy land, covered by broad
stretches of shallow lakes or seas—the landscape of the dino-
saur—has more usually prevailed. The present situation has
recurred again and again down through the aeons of time, but
each such appearance has been brief, bringing to an end
some much longer stage in the evolution or development
of life.

What caused the land to shake itself and rise higher above
the level of the sea, what forces lifted the great mountains
and produced such paroxysms of volcanic activity, are as yet
imperfectly understood. But once these events occur, the air
bred over the continents becomes strikingly different from that

68

resting on the oceans. As a result, extremes of seasonal climate and rapid alterations in the cycle of the weather have been characteristic of those comparatively short geological periods similar to our own.

When the surface of the land lay low and wet, maritime and continental air must have been much the same. Lacking those areas which would heat up severely in summer or cool off correspondingly in winter, the northern half of the world, which contains most of the continental masses, possessed a climate which was even, equable and much warmer toward the North Pole than it is today.

Probably the height of the land was only one of the factors accounting for those changes in climate which can be read in the history of the sedimentary rocks. One of the simplest explanations is that the axis of the planet stood more nearly vertical during these periods, so that there was then little difference in the seasons. In any event, when temperate conditions reached up into the Arctic Circle, there must have been some meteorologically more efficient machinery for transferring heat from the equator, where it is being steadily gained, to the poles, where it is being lost to outer space.

Urged on by the winds of the maritime high pressure areas, the ocean currents, like a giant heating system, circulate warm water to the higher latitudes and bring back cold to be reheated by the sun. A second mechanism for abstracting heat from one part of the earth and carrying it to another is the cycle by which warm air evaporates water from the oceans and then moving elsewhere surrenders its stolen store of energy in the formation of clouds.

The vertical circulation which takes place today in many parts of the world's atmosphere can only carry such tropical heat a third of the way to the pole. As the air rises upwards, towering clouds quickly form close above the spot where the air was initially heated. At the horse latitudes the dry upper winds start sinking down toward the surface, thence to flow back to the equator where their circuit is completed.

When a winter thaw reaches up into Canada, on the other hand, the warm air is moving parallel to the surface of the earth. In such horizontal circulation, clouds form more slowly, hundreds or thousands of miles distant from the spot where their moisture was initially acquired. The energy stolen in the tropics is thus carried over enormous distances. This situation exists today where the Atlantic high, working in co-operation with its partner, the Gulf Stream, gives Scotland a comparatively temperate climate, although it is as far north as Labrador.

The difference between the two forms of circulation carries over into the clouds formed in each type. As warm moist air rises vertically, its water vapor condenses quickly, whereupon the extra heat liberated encourages further ascent. As a result, individual updrafts occur and the clouds become tumbled, billowing and towering. They are named *cumulus,* from the same Latin stem that gives us "accumulate," and range all the way from the rounded wool packs of a fine clear day to the overpowering majesty of a spreading thunderhead.

Contrariwise, when a great mass of moist air moves across the earth's surface horizontally from warm to colder latitudes, it is cooled as a whole slowly. When in due course this cooling has progressed far enough, clouds will form, steadily and in even layers throughout the air's mass. As its water vapor thus condenses, the heat, abstracted from the tropic seas of its homeland, is given up equally gently and consistently. Appearing throughout the whole level of cloud, this supply of extra energy counteracts the cooling effect, and in this way a warm, continuous covering of condensing moisture covers the cooler land below. The clouds so formed are much like elevated banks of fog. Such sheets are called *stratus,* since from top to bottom they consist of an even, continuous layer.

In the dependency of all living things on the heat of the sun, the clouds serve a further function. They can behave either like a blanket or an awning. About the equator, where the world is a steady gainer of solar energy, clouds act to reflect the sun's rays and reduce the amount of heat received at the surface. Towards the poles, on the other hand, the earth is constantly losing heat. Here a thick layer of tiny particles of ice or water helps to reduce the radiation of such energy to outer space.

The vertical circulation of the atmosphere produces much cumulus cloud in the tropics and clear air to north and south. This in turn tends to chill the higher latitudes. A horizontal circulation produces an opposite effect. It sweeps warm moist air away from the central band of the world, leaving the tropic sky clear to the incoming sunlight, and carries the winds far north and south to cover those colder parts of the earth's surface with a thick blanket of warm stratus cloud.

A temperate age in the earth's climatic history seems to have required a vast act of co-operation between the geography, geology and meteorology of our planet. Low land and few mountain ranges would permit the tropic winds freely to circulate across the oceans into the arctic regions. Under these circumstances the atmosphere's horizontal circulation would have been favored at the expense of its vertical.

Such periods of warmth have apparently lasted much longer down the world's span of life than has our present era of climatic extremes. For a climate to ensue such as exists today, the world must first have passed through a relatively short period of stress and strain, during which the continents were lifted and great mountains thrust upward. Perhaps as the earth lay low and swampy century after century, the moving air was slowly stripped of the sandy dust which encourages the fall of rain. Such precipitation might then have been

71

concentrated over the great land masses of what are now Siberia and northern Canada.

If once in these areas the winter snows began to build up faster than they were melted off in summer, science is convinced that such a process could have become self-perpetuating. Retreating as the sun rose high in the heavens, but always advancing further during each long polar night, the sheets of frozen water would expand and deepen year after year.

Slowly but steadily these enormous glaciers and beds of ice would exert a growing pressure on the earth's core. At last the solid crust would have been forced to move and shake in response to the new distribution of the weight of its water. As the land then split and shifted, a period of volcanic activity would have ensued, supplying the air with a new supply of ash and dust to act as sublimation nuclei.

The mountain ranges and the higher, drier land would stimulate the vertical circulation of the atmosphere. As a result the age of ice would be further encouraged; the climatic extremes between equator and poles grow steadily greater.

Much of the above account, to be truthful, is largely speculative. It fails, for example, to account for the curious interglacial periods when a milder climate returned for a while to the world. All the puzzles that exist in the story of the rocks have not been solved; many of the riddles concerning the atmosphere are still unread. Yet where once geology, geography and meteorology were taught as largely separate sciences, they are seen today to be a single entity in tracing the story of the earth's development and in the larger puzzle of how life first came to exist upon its surface.

II

Clouds are the most diverse, the most beautiful and the most manifest of all the different phases or aspects of the weather. Their beauty is best appreciated late in the day, when their outlines are colored by the light of the sinking sun, filtered through the invisible dust of the atmosphere. Their diversity ranges from dull overcast to bright puffball, from filmy lace to threatening thundercloud. And finally they reveal the movements of the air, telling what is taking place below the horizon, what winds are moving aloft and what is the nature and condition of the atmosphere above our heads.

As the sun comes close to the edge of the earth its fingers of light color the clouds, cataloguing them by a succession of deepening tints. Yellow is the stain applied to the lowest clouds. These are the stratus, whose flat even outlines stay within six or seven thousand feet of the surface. These clouds are the products of a gentle, uniform cooling of large parcels of air. Like a fog bank lifted aloft they range from a few hundred to several thousand feet in thickness. When such clouds are modified by vertical currents, or contrariwise, where clouds of the cumulus variety have settled in more stable air, stratus becomes *stratocumulus*. These have a rounded or rolling underside, generally marked by distinct shading from white to gray. In winter they are usually produced as cold stratus overruns some warmer land to the south, while in summer cumulotype clouds moving north will cool to form stratocumulus.

As the sun settles on the horizon its rays next illuminate the middle clouds, coloring them a strong, glorious gold. As the light moves higher, this color deepens to brilliant orange, since these clouds of the intermediate altitudes range in height from seven to twenty thousand feet. In their upper levels they can produce the twilight afterglow, when at first the darkness deepens, and then with the sun in the right position over the rim of the earth its rays are suddenly reflected from such a bank of *altostratus* or *altocumulus*. For a brief space thereafter the light returns, coloring the world for several lovely minutes a surprising golden rose.

73

The middle clouds are of two sorts, depending on whether they have been produced in stable or unstable air, either by a slow lifting or as a result of some vertical currents. Alto-cumulus is the true mackerel sky, scaly and only lightly shaded. Its elements, indicating the effect of what updrafts have co-operated in its formation, are sometimes arranged in lines or waves. In appearance it can merge into its partner, the altostratus. This is more a veil of fibrous fog, bluish gray in color, through which, when it is thin, the sun shines faintly, or when thick, the cloud appears as if lighted from within.

As the sun sinks further out of sight, its light moves on, ranging higher in the atmosphere. Passing through greater and greater thicknesses of the faint dust high overhead, the tint strengthens to fiery red as it touches the highest clouds of all. These are the *cirrus,* from the Latin word for a curl or a lock of hair, consisting of a faint haze or tracery of ice crystals, lying anywhere from four to seven miles aloft.

These clouds are all products of great vertical movements or liftings of the air. Swept upward at the top of a thunder-storm or pushed steadily aloft by fierce struggles along the polar front, they consist of three types. A sheer handkerchief or film of cloud is the *cirrostratus.* So thin it may give only a milky look to the sky, it—like the altostratus—can produce the ring or halo about sun or moon that forecasts the nearer approach of the storm over the horizon which projected the cloud to these great heights. When thicker it can reflect the sunset's fading light as if the sky were on fire, burning with brilliant flame.

Its sister is the *cirrocumulus.* Marked by faint ripples or scallops, like those on wind-blown sand, it retains this weak evidence of the strong vertical currents by which it was produced. As cirrocumulus evaporates or disintegrates, the scales may become separated, showing clear sky between. Or like altocumulus it can be modified into faint ripples or fibrous patches of congealed vapor.

In this form it becomes indistinguishable from cirrus itself, the highest, the most varied and most beautiful of all. As the light in the sky fades more and more, these last clouds are tinted a deeper and deeper red. As isolated tufts or branching plumes or featherlike bands apparently converging toward the horizon, they mark the roof of the atmosphere and brush the ceiling of the weather.

So the sunset's pageant draws to its close. As the darkness grows, only the faint purple of the atmospheric dust shows in a half circle around the earth's rim. Overhead the deep blue of night grows stronger, as the first bright star suddenly appears to the casual, wandering eye.

III

In the catalogue of the clouds the wide diversity of forms which are covered by the name of cumulus require space to themselves. Occurring within shafts of air which are ascending vertically upward, they assume their tufted, rolling outline as each current is then encouraged to move on upwards by the heat given up in such condensation. The conditions out of which they arise range all the way from the stiff, bumpy updrafts of a warm clear day in late spring to the wicked up and down currents that boil within a summer thunderstorm.

Such clouds as these form as the sun heats up the land unequally during the daylight hours. They occur within an individual air mass and are therefore sometimes called air-mass clouds, in distinction to the same type when they are formed as part of a frontal battle. Billowing cumulus clouds are likewise produced when the strong chill shoulder of a cold front pushes hot, moist air violently upward. A steep mountain range, facing the prevailing winds from a warm ocean, acts exactly similarly. Both lift the air so rapidly to the condensation level that thereafter it takes off under the power of its own rapidly produced heat.

When cold air moves down in a mass from the north, its levels are generally stable. Cool in its lower reaches, its temperature falls off comparatively slowly in its upper levels. In spring the land it overruns may be warming up rapidly. The mounting sun can then supply sufficient additional heat so that the wheeling buzzards will be seen gliding steadily in the resulting updrafts. When these thermal currents rise to the condensation level, each becomes topped with its individual tufted plume of cloud. With their bases all occurring at one level, their tops likewise are apt to be all in a plane, as the heavy hand of the cold air's stability aloft prevents the rising currents from moving higher.

This white procession of woolly sheep comprises the *fair weather cumulus* or *cumulus humilis*. As they move out of the west they tell the ground-rooted observer that the air above them is dry and stable, that they will disappear with the darkness as the land cools, and that the night will be clear and cold.

A different set of conditions arises when moist warm air moves northward in summer. As the sun's full force develops around midday, such air starts ascending, quickly reaching the condensation level. Encouraged by the heat evolved in the formation of each cloud, the individual currents push higher into the unstable atmosphere. By early afternoon the ground is continuing to grow hotter, and several separate updrafts may concentrate in some growing focus of vertical activity. The shading of the mounting clouds becomes more and more contrasting, ranging from brilliant white to dark ominous black, their billowing outline evidencing their inner turbulence.

Such clouds are *cumulus congestus,* the well-named *con-*

gested cumulus. They are the typical clouds of the tropical rainy season and of the passing cold front. From them as the afternoon wears on in the middle latitudes a summer thunderstorm may develop. If it does, its further growth more and more depends on the heat building up internally from the large amount of invisible moisture forming into visible cloud. As the cloud mass grows greater, its top assumes the appearance of a gigantic cauliflower, tumbling visibly upwards fifteen to thirty thousand feet overhead.

At these altitudes the winds of the upper air sweep some of the lifted cloud, like a streaming pennant, in the direction of their flow. Above the cauliflower head and out of its center an anvil shape appears, its point pointing with the winds aloft. This is a cloud of pure ice crystals and is a sign that somewhere within the violent up and down drafts rain is forming. This does not mean necessarily that as yet any precipitation is falling out of the base of the clouds.

So fiercely are the vertical currents moving that they can tear apart the individual raindrops, leaving their separate halves charged with opposite elements of electricity. Forces of electrical attraction and repulsion are thus added to the whirling thermal action. This unbalance continues until it is at last relieved by the discharge of static electricity which we see as lightning, the readjustment of the atmosphere being evidenced by the attendant clap of thunder.

Within a mass of cumulus congestus, the formation of ice crystals gives the water droplets something rapidly to grow on. Therefore as soon as a tuft of cirrus appears at its top, the clouds mass is called *cumulonimbus,* the *cumulus raincloud.* In the tropics rain falls in many cases without the formation of such microscopic snowflakes, and this may be true in our latitudes as well. But the appearance of a plume of cirrus is always proof positive that the process of precipitation has commenced.

Such precipitation is generally in the form of heavy rain, but at times it may consist of the rattle of hail. This is not the result of water vapor changing directly into the solid state; only snow forms its lovely crystalline structure in this way. Instead hail is the result of rain freezing as water is frozen to a cube of ice in the household refrigerator. In a thunderstorm some rain is often swept into an updraft, at the top of which it is then congealed.

Such a summer storm is not actually a single entity. Instead it is an assemblage of many individual vertical currents. Below each particular mass of congested cumulus, a central pillar of air is usually descending within a circular shaft of ascending air. Together, below a mounting thunderhead, these rush violently upwards and down in close and turbulent proximity. Sometimes large hailstones will be found to look rather like onions, each of their several skins attesting to an upward trip through the storm's freezing level.

In addition to being produced by the heat of the mounting sun, congested cumulus can be caused by moist incoming air which has to rise above a mountain range. The rising land lifts the air rapidly to the condensation level, whereupon if the air contains enough water and if the further levels of the atmosphere are sufficiently unstable, the formation of the clouds will itself engender the heat necessary to produce further vertical movement and the clouds will tower upwards, rising indeed under their own steam.

A cold front operates similarly, but since it is a moving rather than a stationary obstacle to the moist air, the violence of its passage will depend on how fast the front is moving and how different is its own air from that which it is lifting. When the conditions are extreme, a cold front will produce the surprise of a thunderstorm in the middle of winter. Such storms when they occur, however, generally take place high overhead. Dangerous as they are to the aviator trying to fly through the long and often continuous line of squall and turbulence, to those on the ground they seldom present the same hazards as the air-mass thunderstorm. The lightning only in exceptional cases strikes vertically from cloud to earth; instead the atmospheric balance is redressed by a stroke which shoots horizontally from cloud to cloud.

Planes have unwittingly flown into thunderstorms, but the experience is not habit-forming. Terrible turbulence is encountered around the center, vertical velocities of 200 miles per hour being measured by those who were fortunate enough to come out alive. Today specially built aircraft, equipped with the latest instruments and devices, are studying the thunderstorm and its big brother, the hurricane. Out of their dangerous investigations will come an expansion of man's knowledge of how water operates with heat to produce these great atmospheric vortices.

IV

During the cool clear nights of autumn a miniature example of the formation of cloud is the fog that settles in lowland or valley. With no wind to disturb it, heavy cold air drains down the slopes and hillsides, coming to rest over the dampness of swamp or pond or stream. Unprotected by a blanket of cloud overhead, the air radiates away the heat acquired during the day, and in those pockets where it can sink no further, chills to the dew point.

These patchy autumn fogs are generally shallow and soon disappear with the next morning's sun. The great fog banks of the seacoast, on the other hand, are formed like their cousin, the stratus cloud, when moist warm air is as a whole slowly and uniformly chilled. Such blankets of fog occur in winter over Texas and the Southeast, when air from the Gulf moves slowly inland over the cold ground.

During the summer, fog forms similarly over the Grand Banks, where the hot wet air from the Gulf Stream is chilled by the cold waters of the Labrador Current. Just north of the Golden Gate is one of those spots in the ocean where from its depths cold water wells up mysteriously to the surface. As a result, summer air from the Pacific high overrunning this chilly area brings cold fog to San Francisco and Seattle when the rest of the country is apt to be sweltering in a summer heat wave.

In the Middle West the land rises gently toward the peaks of the Rockies. Like the cold air below an advancing warm front, the land here forms a ramp up which air from the southeast is lifted steadily and slowly. At the condensation level, fog blankets the ground, occurring in the same way as stratus clouds are usually formed aloft. Like the white veils of mist that at times hide the mountain peaks, such fog is simply a cloud that has come down to touch the ground.

With the morning light a layer of fog often appears as if it were being burned away by the sun. Indeed, solar heat is the enemy of all stratoform clouds. As the temperature rises, their component droplets start evaporating one by one, the warming air changing increasing amounts of their moisture into water vapor. Unless it is blown away by the wind, fog only returns to invisibility by being warmed from below or heated from above. Cloud, however, riding the air aloft, can sink to its own destruction into warmer levels that lie below it.

During the day the sun's heat steadily stimulates the rising currents at the top of which cumulus cloud can form. With nightfall these thermal updrafts have ceased to rise and the air is busy sorting itself out into its natural levels of pressure and temperature. A cloud caught in this process may then appear to be eaten by the rising moon. Fair weather cumulus or the clouds left over from an afternoon thunderstorm sink slowly to a lower level, as the atmosphere adjusts itself to the sun's departure. At this new altitude of warmer temperature and greater pressure their droplets begin to evaporate and the clouds in time may completely disappear.

Wind is the second enemy of fog. With a gentle breeze the air moves as a whole, but once its velocity attains sufficient force, eddies and turbulence are set up which bring in new air to mix with that which is becoming saturated. Both fog and clouds are shredded away into patches by high winds, to become the seaman's scud or by the experts to be assigned the prefix *fracto*, from the Latin word for broken.

The sudden advent of fog is a great hazard to aviation. The makers of artificial rain have succeeded in dissipating such restrictions to visibility by seeding them with silver iodide or dry ice. Unfortunately, however, the trick seems to work properly only when the temperature of the mist is below that of freezing.

Unsatisfactory as this result is to aviators, it throws considerable light on the completion of the three-stage cycle of evaporation, condensation and precipitation. The work of the rain makers indicates that the formation of rain or snow from a stratus cloud starts in those levels where its drops are super-cooled. The necessary growth in the size of the individual droplets must be triggered by the presence of ice crystals or by a mixing of cloud at different temperatures. Then, once gravity gets a firm hold of a tiny sphere of water or a growing flake of snow, the falling particles will pick up additional moisture as they fall through the layers of cloud below them.

When precipitation starts falling out of the base of a stratoform cloud, it is called the *nimbostratus,* the stratus rain cloud. Breaking a summer drought the rain falls steadily in small drops, allowing the life-restoring moisture ample time to sink into the parched ground. In winter such clouds bring the fine powdery snow which although a foot high weighs less than the shovel, a scourge to the householder but a joy to those enthusiasts who plunge down the mountain slopes with their feet idiotically clamped to long wooden boards.

V

Although it is easy to write down clear-cut definitions and exact descriptions on paper, the clouds as they move overhead change slowly and imperceptibly from one kind into another. Except legally, it is equally hard to determine when a boy has become a man. So likewise it is difficult, if not impossible, to say where stratus changes to altostratus or when cirrocumulus has lowered sufficiently to become altocumulus.

These precise distinctions are obviously matters for the expert. To the amateur a knowledge of the different forms of cloud is primarily for the purpose of increasing his enjoyment in living and his ability to associate himself with the natural environment in which he exists. In such terms the catalogue of the clouds can well begin with the separation into those which are formed in heavy, stable air and those produced by thermally ascending currents; that is, into stratoform and cumulo-type.

The beginner will find it easy to distinguish the fair weather cumulus humilis from the towering cumulus congestus. In the first, the updrafts are occurring in comparatively dry northern air, while the other is mounting upwards through levels of the atmosphere whose properties were probably acquired over some warm, distant sea. If toward the horizon he sees a mass of congested cumulus raising its cauliflower head and forming a great anvil at its top, he will look for the feathery plume of ice crystals that will tell him a thunderstorm is in progress and that the cloud form has become cumulonimbus.

A second grouping of the clouds is by their altitudes. A certain amount of experience is necessary to judge if a cloud lies in the low, middle or upper reaches of the troposphere,

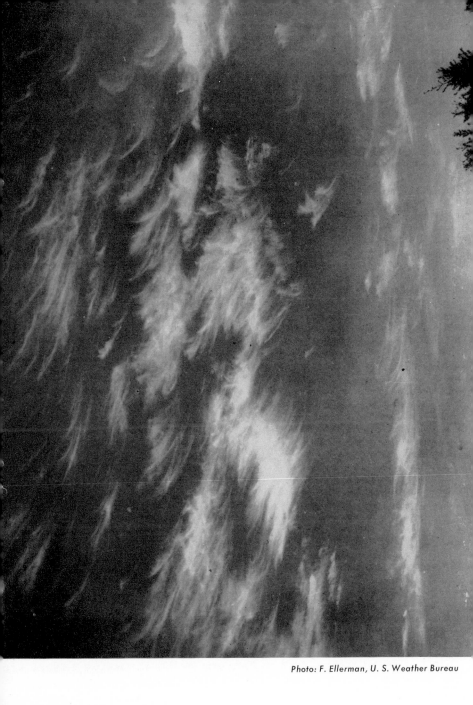

Photo: F. Ellerman, U. S. Weather Bureau

I.

Cirrus

Photo: L. A. Boyd, U. S. Weather Bureau

II.

Cirrostratus

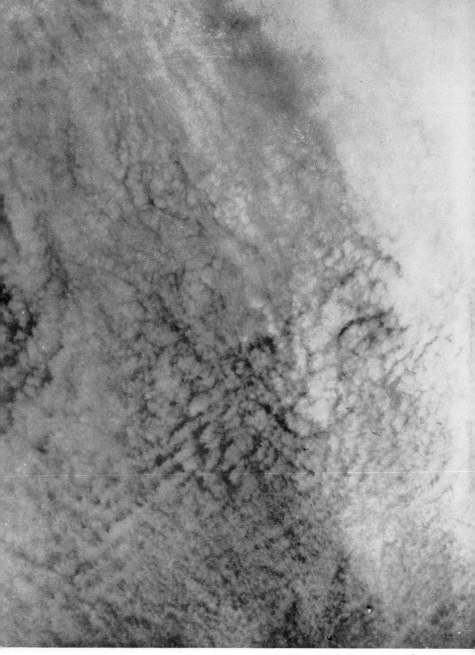

Photo: H. T. Floreen, U. S. Weather Bureau

III.

Cirrocumulus

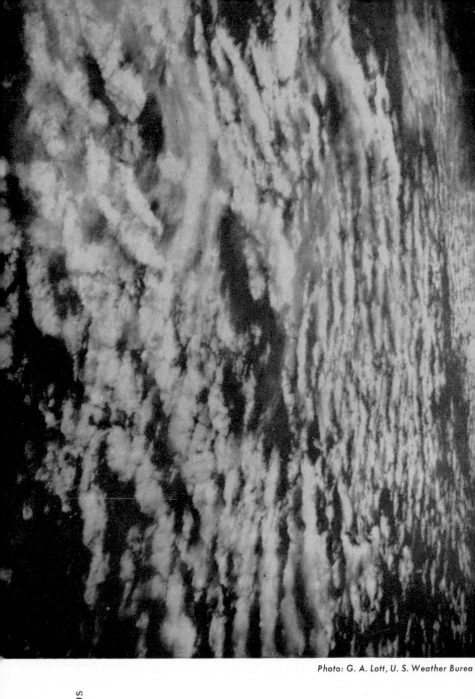

Photo: G. A. Lott, U. S. Weather Burea

IV.

Altocumulus

Photo: U. S. Weather Bureau

V.

Altostratus
above. Fog
and Stratus
below

VI.
Nimbostratus,
thinning to
Altostratus
towards the
horizon

Photo: W. J. Humphreys, U. S. Weather Bureau

VII. Stratocumulus

VIII.
Cumulus in
various stages
of develop-
ment

Photo: H. T. Floreen, U. S. Weather Bureau

but a precise determination is hardly necessary to the amateur meteorologist. In the first place he will have little trouble with the lowest clouds, the stratus, the stratocumulus and their brother raincloud, the nimbostratus. These are composed entirely of water droplets and look like a bank of fog or mist, which is what in fact they are.

Lying between 6,500 and 20,000 feet, the clouds of the middle levels are the difficult ones to identify accurately. Like many intermediate forms, they merge imperceptibly into the ones immediately above and below them. They are, to be sure, of only two types, the altostratus and the altocumulus. Yet in their lowest positions they are entirely water clouds, while in their highest altitudes they are composed solely of ice crystals. In between they are usually made up of a mixture of water particles in both the solid and liquid state. They are therefore of great technical interest to those who are trying to puzzle out exactly how precipitation gets started.

The clouds of the middle levels often show how the air is moving aloft. In their highest position there is little to differentiate them from those which are called cirrus. But these last clouds which reach up and brush the base of the stratosphere are clearly in a class by themselves. Formed by meteorological forces of vast scope and considerable violence, these, in their assemblage of pure ice crystals, are the end products of conflict, storm and strife. When produced at the top of the gentle ramp of a warm front, they are seen as cirrostratus, while if boiled up out of a strong cold front or at the top of tumbling cumulonimbus, they will appear as cirrocumulus. Their fate is never to return to lower levels. Lifted as lacy feathers or plumes, disintegrating into faint patches or streaks, the cirrus eventually evaporates to supply the top of the troposphere with the slight trace of water vapor which is all that these cold, thin layers can hold.

CHAPTER VI

The Wind Bloweth Where It Listeth

I

IT is provoking in an age of science to realize how many natural facts are taken on faith. That the earth spins on its axis, that it revolves in an orbit around the central sun, that the planets like the moon shine by reflected light and are much nearer than the distant stars, all these are taught to school children and become a part of their basic thinking about nature. But many well-educated people might find it troublesome to explain these matters to a skeptical Hottentot or would experience considerable difficulty in assembling the necessary tangible evidence to demonstrate that the solar system operates in the way they learned at school.

During various periods in the past, views entirely contrary to those now held were authoritatively taught, probably to equally bored and uncritical students. All during the Middle Ages the earth was firmly placed at the center of the celestial system. Well into the seventeen hundreds many scientists contended that heat was a substance. They called it *phlogiston* and considered it as tangible a thing as the molecules of matter. At the beginning of the previous century the whole question of atmospheric pressure was simply dismissed by the ancient dictum that nature abhors a vacuum.

In that transference of interest from the artistic and aesthetic to the mathematical and scientific which marked the second stage of the Renaissance, a young Italian devised the means to measure nature's real attitude towards any reduction in the atmospheric pressure. During the last years of his life, the great Galileo was living quietly in Florence under the watchful but indulgent eye of the Church, which had objected to the way he had been mixing science with theology. Failing eyesight required him to employ a secretary who also had to possess some knowledge of natural philosophy. The young Torricelli, to be sure, never equaled his master, but he became a first-rate mathematician and scientist in his own right and gave the world the tube which is still the most accurate instrument for measuring a partial vacuum.

A goal is of course an admirable thing in life. To the bickering princes of Renaissance Europe, the ability to refill their perennially empty treasuries by the transmutation of some cheaper metal into silver or gold was certainly a worth-while objective. That the alchemists were unsuccessful is only secondary to the point that they failed in adding much to human knowledge largely because they were too closely concerned with a practical matter.

The newer generation of scientists and mathematicians was making no such mistake as this. Just as art had flourished for men who were naturally delighted by color and form, so a new group of men was taking simple pleasure in breaking down a beam of sunlight into its rainbow of colors or puzzling out what force was producing an unexpected jerk in the legs of a dead frog.

In these investigations and researches, as part of these nosings and questings that were largely without any practical purpose, one group of men was busy designing and constructing a range of new instruments and devices. With these novel scientific toys the scientifically curious were enabled to observe many facts in nature never before seen or noted.

One such optical instrument, when pointed at the heavens, demolished, before Galileo's eye, one of the cornerstones of the

85

theory that the earth was at the center of the universe. Another, using similar principles, showed to an excitable Dutchman that life existed in teeming quantities in every drop of the ditch water of his flat, sandy countryside.

What these eager, scientific mechanics furnished Torricelli was a simple thing, a length of air-tight pipe. With it he established, in 1643, the extent to which nature really abhorred a vacuum. The result seemed clearly fixed and was definitely measurable. In such a container, closed at the top and open at the bottom, water would stand at thirty-four feet. The force that was holding the liquid upright was, in Torricelli's view, the pressure of the atmosphere. But perhaps there was some other explanation; perhaps this was some special property of water itself.

Gold being one of the heaviest metals, most alchemists had worked with lead. But there was another school which preferred to begin with *quicksilver,* that heavy, shiny liquid which appears in the modern catalogue of elements as mercury. When a three-foot glass tube, filled with this material, was closed at one end and then upended with its open end in a dish, the mercury consistently stood upright some thirty inches high. Since this height of quicksilver possesses the same weight as thirty-four feet of water, the young scientific world of the day was ready to accept the new fact that the atmosphere was exerting upon the earth a pressure of some fifteen pounds per square inch.

No doubt a healthy, well-conditioned whale would resent being suddenly told that he lived in a wet, cold, uncomfortable environment. So the average seventeenth century European was acutely displeased with the idea that he was existing, and had been since birth, subject to a pressure which he had never felt and from which he had never experienced the slightest discomfort. Such a suggestion, the more conservative asserted, was dangerous, radical and probably a serious threat to the foundations of church and state.

On the scientific level, too, the matter seemed questionable. The mercury within its sealed tube had a curious trick of changing its height, which hardly seemed consistent with any sort of constant pressure. Such variations might be similar to the regular movements of the tides. But unfortunately the motion, which amounted to more than two inches, could not be related to any known natural rhythms.

Annoyed by this aberration in his new instrument, as well as by the gibes of the nonbelievers in his theory, Torricelli at length obtained a correlation that was clear-cut, albeit totally unexpected. A drop in the mercury in his tube uncannily foretold a worsening in the weather, while its rise generally forecast a corresponding improvement.

To human health and comfort this was a much more useful result than the one the alchemists were seeking. But in scientific progress the practical is largely a by-product. What had occurred—with the invention of an instrument to measure changes in the atmospheric pressure—was the birth of the science of meteorology.

II

Time may or may not prove to be some manifestation of a fourth dimension, but it certainly operates to increase the difficulty with which the human mind assembles its thoughts or its imaginings. Like motion, time is something the mind prefers to reject by bringing everything to a stop. Thus pressure is easiest thought of as a push, suction as a pull. Unfortunately such a simple picture of a static force is not adequate to describe the changes in the atmospheric pressure which occur as the air moves within the troposphere.

It is of course true that any gas moves upward when it is

warmed and therefore light, that contrariwise it sinks downward if it is cold and hence heavy. But it is not solely the lightness of one such atmospheric parcel or the heaviness of another that causes the rise or fall in Torricelli's tube of mercury. Like the water from a garden hose, any movement in a gas or liquid produces a force which is itself felt as a push or a pull.

A fall in the barometer occurs not only because the air is statically lighter, but because it is likewise moving dynamically upward. It is the air itself which lifts part of its own weight from the surface of the earth. At the base of the stratosphere this situation is reversed. Here, seven or eight miles overhead, the mounting air is held down by the ceiling of the weather. Unable to push on through the warmer layers above it, the air can only raise this invisible barrier into a gigantic mushroom, beneath which it is then forced to flow away sideways.

Here therefore the air backs up and becomes relatively dense. At these extreme altitudes most of the atmosphere lies earthward, so that the quicksilver would stand only a few inches high in its glass. But as compared to other areas at the same height above the ground, this will be a spot of comparative high pressure.

Such a topsy-turvy situation of low pressure on the ground and high pressure aloft is reversed in those localities where the air is sinking downward. Here the top of the troposphere dips into an immense dimple, indicating the lower pressure produced by the air descending below it. On the ground the gaseous molecules, as they move to lower levels, become an extra weight that must be supported by the air close to the surface.

Reacting to the vertical circulation of the atmosphere, the top of the troposphere is not a simple spherical shell. Instead the weather's roof rises highest at the equator, dips over the horse latitudes, then is lifted again above the polar front and sinks finally lowest over the poles. In the vertical movements which cause these alterations, the motion of the air and the pressure of the atmosphere act as partners, one reinforcing and supporting the behavior of the other. Moving through only a few thousand feet, however, they operate over relatively short distances as compared to the hundreds of thousands of miles of horizontal flow which we feel as wind.

A simple picture of such lateral motion would be a firm push out of an area of high pressure, encouraged by the welcoming pull into one where the barometer is falling. This to be sure is the way the air is urged to travel as it moves parallel to the ground. But as to a stroller in a public park, the atmosphere has its own signs saying KEEP OFF THE GRASS, which effectively prevent it from moving directly across lots, from high to low.

A straight line, geometry asserts, is the shortest distance between two points. Across a sphere, however, there are no straight lines; on the level surface of the earth anyone moving straight ahead covers a portion of a gigantic circle. In addition, our planet is spinning on its axis. Moving at only moderate speeds a ship at sea or the automobile rolling down the highway does not feel the effect of this daily rotation. But to the shell of a twelve-inch gun or to the jet-propelled aircraft, a curved path above a spinning globe produces an apparent force which thrusts it always to the right in the northern hemisphere, to the left in the southern.

The complicated thing about this deflection is that it operates independently of the direction. It can be visualized most easily if one simply thinks of some object traveling rapidly north or south into an area where the earth is moving faster or slower than at the point of departure. But with enough mathematics, proof can be adduced that the earth will spin out below any moving thing, no matter in what direction it is headed.

89

With or without mathematical reasoning, the coriolus force is a definite fact, for which artillerymen must compensate and for which navigators of aircraft must allow. Near the equator it is negligible, reaching its maximum at the poles. In addition, the faster an object moves the greater the distance it will cover in a given time and equally the greater will be the amount of the earth's surface which has moved beneath it.

This is the strait jacket that is imposed on the winds which blow about the earth. Any such air, urged on by a push from some area of high pressure or feeling the pull from one where the barometer is low, finds itself forced to follow a curved path. The winds may then rise as they attempt to iron out such differences in the atmospheric pressure. But as the earth spins steadily on its axis, the air's increased speed will only set it into a more determinedly circular path, will force it more firmly to curve round Robin Hood's barn, on a road which is characteristic of how wind and pressure work together in all the varying meteorological moods which in the middle latitudes make up the kaleidoscope of our weather.

III

Palm Beach, Miami, and the other towns of Florida's east coast are the nation's winter playground. With the sun standing well south of the equator, their beaches are warmed by the clear dry air descending from high below the stratosphere. Except when an occasional heavy thrust from the cold north nips the citrus groves or chills the lightly dressed vacationers, their weather in winter is ideal.

In the summer, on the other hand, the climate along Florida's west coast is much to be preferred. At this time of year, the land by day becomes hotter than the water on both sides of the peninsula, while at night it cools quickly to a lower temperature. As a result the air is sucked inland daily, while at night it reverses its flow and moves toward the sea. Overriding this daily alternation blow the trade winds from the direction of Bermuda.

On the east coast the sea breeze during the day moves with the prevailing wind, but by midnight the air is apt to become still and stifling. Trying to move as a land breeze out to sea, it meets the trade winds head on and produces substantially an atmospheric stalemate. On the west coast, however, this situation is reversed. The sea breeze of the daytime may make the afternoons a little sultry, but at night the land breeze and the prevailing winds co-operate in a strong, cooling flow.

The wind off the ocean by day and from the land by night are familiar changes along many tropical seacoasts. They result simply from differences in temperatures between contrasting surfaces of the earth. The example on the largest scale of this rhythm is the seasonal monsoon winds of Asia, but many other cases exist about the world. One of the best known is the *mistral* of southern France, which blows across the Mediterranean into the hot furnace of the Sahara. Such winds move, largely within the tropics and with little deflection, from an area of high pressure towards one where the barometer is correspondingly low, from some spot where the air is cooling and sinking to some other area where it is hot and rising.

In contrast to these local movements which are marked by a daily or seasonal alternation are the winds resulting from the general circulation of the atmosphere. These consist of three bands in each hemisphere: the Trade Winds, the Prevailing Westerlies and the Polar Easterlies. Such broad belts of diagonally moving air result from the three main vertical movements within the troposphere. But they are in turn broken up by the horizontal whirlpools of air which occur primarily because of the geographic distribution of land and sea across the world.

From the rims of these permanent centers of high or low pressure, masses of air spin off to produce the struggle along the polar front. This conflict moves generally from west to east, but within each air mass or as part of the storms their battle engenders, the direction of flow swings all around the clock. These winds have a pattern of behavior that is all their own, causing them to sweep in great curved paths as each mass of air surges onward unopposed or is buffeted in conflict with some rival. But such movements of the atmosphere that make manifest the force of the weather operate hand in hand with otherwise unfelt, delicate adjustments in the barometric pressure.

Where air is moving vertically downward, the barometer will stand highest. In all directions from this center of high pressure the air at the surface will be trying to move outwards. Similarly, the mercury in Torricelli's tube will fall if it is moved across the surface of the earth and away from the area where the air is sinking. For the first fifty or one hundred miles the height of the quicksilver will drop slowly, but as it gets out from under the main column of descending air it will move downward steadily and evenly with each additional distance that it is moved out and away.

The level of the barometer, as it is moved about within an area where the air is sinking toward the surface, can be imagined as describing a sort of vast, circular hillock. Highest at the center below the area where the air is primarily descending, this synthetic mound slopes more and more steeply downward out where the winds are blowing parallel to the ground. Following these contours, it would seem logical to imagine that the air would move outward like water flowing down an actual hillside.

Curiously enough, the winds blow not across but essentially parallel to these contours of pressure. As the air at first moves outward from the center, it is seized upon by the deflecting force, the apparent impulse imposed upon it by the spin of the globe. Urged to the right in the northern hemisphere, the winds move onward faster and faster as the slope of the pressure grows steeper and steeper.

But growing with their increasing speed, the strength of the coriolus force binds the winds into a circle, so that their increasing velocity avails them nothing. Except at the surface where friction with the ground allows them to move outward, the winds, which might be expected to move like curved spokes of a wheel, act instead more as a succession of hoops binding in the central power of the descending air.

IV

The deflecting force which thrusts at all the winds blowing about the world is produced by the rotation of the earth on its axis. Although the mathematics required to demonstrate its existence is indeed complicated, a simple experiment will show how our planet's spin effects another sort of movement. The equipment is simple, consisting of fifteen or twenty feet of rope, a substantial weight of fifty or a hundred pounds and a swivel or collar to attach the first two to a high beam or rafter.

If the weight is suspended from the rope and set swinging like a pendulum, the only further requirement is that the whole apparatus should be sufficiently free of friction so that it will continue to move over a period of several hours. What it will then show at the poles is this: if the weight is started swinging at midday, by six o'clock its sweep will be at right angles to the direction in which it was first set in motion.

At the north pole, where the world spins slowly below one's feet, this result is perhaps easy enough to visualize. But down the bulge of the earth it is considerably harder to picture how the room, in which this experiment is being conducted, continues to turn steadily, albeit more slowly, at a rate which grows less with diminishing latitude. Nevertheless the fact which this simple equipment proves is that the pendulum is moving always along its original straight line, while the building that houses it turns as the earth turns.

When the winds are actually moving straight ahead, they appear to the ground-rooted observer to be following a curved path, as the world spins round below them. Therefore when the weather man finds the air moving straight, relative to the turning earth, he knows that it is feeling some second force, some counteracting thrust, which is preventing it from turning in the direction in which it naturally wants to go.

The pull that at times causes the air to straighten out and apparently fly right is a decrease in the atmospheric pressure, the same sort of variation that three hundred years ago caused Torricelli to doubt the accuracy of his instrument. In our hemisphere this falling off in the level of the barometer must be felt always on the wind's left hand. If it occurred on the other side, on the one in which the air wants to turn, the wind would simply flow in and immediately fill up any such existing partial vacuum.

Where the mercury in the barometer drops, beneath an area in which clouds are forming and rain beginning to fall, the growing atmospheric suction turns the winds into a circular path that the meteorologists call cyclonic. Turning clockwise in the southern hemisphere, counterclockwise in our half of the globe, such an area of low pressure is not simply the opposite of one where the barometer stands naturally high. What is added, where the mercury drops low in its tube, is a steady supply of incoming water vapor, collapsing into the liquid or solid particles that comprise the clouds.

This suction, that counteracts the deflecting force and turns the winds into a cyclonic sweep, is not a simply pictured, static force. Instead, the heat that is surrendered as the clouds form lightens the air and starts it moving dynamically upward. Below any such column of rising air the barometer must drop as this upward movement lifts part of the usual weight of the atmosphere off Torricelli's dish of quicksilver.

Falling in response to the quick violence of a passing thunderstorm, it will go down steadily as one of the storms along the polar front moves in its direction. Reacting similarly within the permanent centers of low pressure around Iceland and the Aleutian Islands, it reserves its lowest readings for the terrible hurricanes spawned along the equator in spring and autumn.

The change of water vapor into cloud and the heat which results must be triggered, paradoxically enough, by some sort of cooling. When the air is sufficiently unstable, as it is when a thunderstorm occurs, a vertically rising current ascends dynamically into colder levels aloft. Another way in which the air can be chilled is when it flows against either a mountain range or else a mass of other, colder air. Its own impetus then carries it up and over the obstruction. Where in this ascent it is lifted to the condensation level, clouds will begin to form, either stratus or cumulus in character, depending on whether the atmosphere here is stable or unstable.

Within any major center of storm or low barometric pressure, one or both these processes will be at work. Around the permanent areas of low pressure at the top of the Atlantic and Pacific, the warm wet air off the oceans is continuously being chilled to the dew point by cold dry air from about the pole. Within the storms in our latitudes a similar conflict, albeit a more temporary one, must occur. In the case of the great tropical hurricanes, about which science does not know as much as it would like, a tongue of cold air, thrusting towards the equator, is thought to start the eventually gigantic process.

In any such area of deepening low pressure, the resulting action is twofold, one vertical and the other horizontal. Near the center the surrendered heat starts the air rising. At the same time, as water vapor condenses into cloud, a force of suction is created which urges the outer winds to flow sideways and inwards.

If Torricelli's tube is imagined as being moved about through a region where the air is thus rising and spinning cyclonically, the changing height of the mercury will mark out a sort of saucer or soup plate. Lowest and flattest around the center, the contours marked out by the moving quicksilver slope upward steadily, until they flatten out eventually into a sort of rim.

Here, far out from the center, the air is moving gently as it feels in our hemisphere the beginnings of a leftward pull. Reacting to this force it turns little by little, more and more cyclonically, picking up speed as it does so. Sweeping around in an inward spiral, it comes to the edge of the rim on the depression's saucer.

This is the point where the winds pick up enough velocity, along a path which is sufficiently curved, to balance the suction which is attempting to pull them inwards. Here, where the barometer begins to drop steadily toward the center, the arrangement of wind and pressure is nicely adjusted. If on the one hand the pull at the center grows greater, the circling air will move inward, but it cannot move far before its greater speed in a tighter circle will counteract the force of the stronger central pull. On the other hand, if this force grows less, the winds simply slow down and move outward a few miles to where a new balance will be established.

Just as they do around an area where the air is heavy and cold, the winds sweeping oppositely about a center of low pressure blow substantially parallel to the contours which mark the height of the barometer. These circling currents behave like a set of elastic bands, adjusting themselves automatically to the changing atmospheric strains that develop as the air towards the center grows warmer and thinner.

By their cushioning action they thus prevent the storm from collapsing upon itself and ensure that it maintains its characteristic activity for several days. Within this outer circuit the surface winds grow weaker and weaker, as closer to the center the motion of the air turns more and more upward. Indeed within the dreaded hurricane there is an eye which is completely calm, where sometimes the sun will shine and where high overhead the warmed air is rising directly towards the base of the stratosphere.

CHAPTER VII

The Wild Blue Yonder

I

THE progress of science is generally represented as being marked by hard work and steady determination; by the clear deductions of exact reasoning plus occasional strokes of high genius. Little is said, however, about another common factor: pure luck. Galvani in the field of electricity and Goodyear in the vulcanizing of rubber, to name two famous examples, made their initial discoveries largely by the immediate help of simple good fortune. Granted that it takes real ability to analyze the unexpected or to uncover its heretofore hidden meaning, yet in science as in so many other walks of life, nature, which usually frowns on all our best efforts, occasionally appears suddenly to smile.

The atomic age was born from a clear case of such happenstance. In 1895, Herr Röntgen discovered a new sort of powerful, penetrating ray. Produced when electricity was forced through a glass tube from which most of the gas had been removed, these X-rays were invisible. But when they struck certain chemical compounds, such secondary materials glowed with visible light. This in turn could be photographed, and it is by this means that our bones are observed beneath their covering of flesh and muscle. This secondary property, however, as well as its close cousin by which the firefly produces its faint glow, had been known for years.

The following year, in Paris, an expert in this older field was testing all the known materials which possessed this characteristic of fluorescence or which he thought might exhibit it. Becquerel's procedure was simple. A thin sheet of the compound to be examined was placed on a photographic plate, the whole wrapped in dark paper to shut out all visible light. This package was then exposed to the sun. If the material was fluorescent, penetrating solar rays would produce this secondary emission and the photographic plate would thereby be fogged or light-struck.

One day, as the samples were being prepared, the sun disappeared behind a bank of cloud. This was the initial piece of good luck. The second was even better. Becquerel in this test was using a compound of the heaviest known element, uranium. A third bit of good fortune then topped the other two.

Routine is for many people an essential part of organized activity. Put away in a drawer, the unexposed samples were nonetheless developed as part of Becquerel's standard procedure. To his astonishment the photographic emulsion showed clear evidence of exposure to light. When Becquerel turned to investigate this totally unexpected occurrence, he discovered that it was a property of the uranium itself and had nothing to do with the fluorescence which he and his father had been studying for years.

As a young Polish chemist and her husband, a French physicist, were shortly to demonstrate, these emanations were part of an actual transmutation of matter. The dream of the alchemists had at last come true. But the end product was certainly not gold, nor could the process be in any way controlled. While with unflagging patience and astonishing precision the Curies concentrated minute quantities of a radically new and active element, they asserted first as a theoretical generalization and then showed as an uncontradictable fact that these changes took place in the heart of the atom, pro-

99

ceeding as relentlessly and uncontrollably as the progress of time.

Such changes in matter, which accompany the emission of the rays that Becquerel had so luckily discovered, were a totally new thing in physical science. But although a new age was in fact born at the turn of the century, the average man throughout the world only became aware of its existence, or at least of all its implications, when fifty years later an enormous cloud mushroomed into the air above a Japanese city.

II

The planes which carried the bomb over Japan were at that time the most finished product of American aeronautical skill. When the first B-29's appeared in the Pacific, naval aviators noted in envious detail their size, their power and the multiplicity of their advanced gadgetry. Along the bars of officers' clubs, which by army standards seemed opulently luxurious, the yarn spread among the fliers who wore wings of gold instead of silver that, included in the equipment of the new Super-Fortresses, was an arm which appeared from beside the pilot's seat and at the completion of a successful mission automatically affixed the Air Medal.

But at first not every mission was successful. With its cabin sealed to maintain a comfortable working pressure for its earth-bred occupants, this first true strategic aircraft was designed to fly at altitudes that reached well up toward the base of the stratosphere. At these levels, its designers anticipated, interception would be difficult, antiaircraft fire ineffective, its bomb run largely unopposed. This evaluation was in the main correct: the first B 29's which arrived over their targets flew much as on a training flight.

Unfortunately at this time meteorology knew all too little

about the atmospheric currents existing in the upper half of the troposphere. In addition to the bugs which beset every new plane in any strange theater of operations, some flights found themselves contending with a force of wind or weather which was thrusting them far off course or setting them back, with dwindling reserves of fuel, well short of their target.

As a result the naval aviators obtained their professionally satisfactory revenge. The army fliers were indoctrinated in the close team play between air and surface craft which had originated in the long retreat out of the Philippines, and which the Navy had then perfected in the advance back across the Pacific.

While dark-gray Dumbo planes circled steadily overhead, submarines surfaced to their call and snatched air crews from yellow life rafts, sometimes within gunshot of the Japanese coast. At the same time, the meteorologists on Guam sweated over their charts and ground out their calculations, seeking an answer to what was happening high in the air over Honshu.

In due course they were forced to recognize that in these upper levels there existed currents which were moving faster than any gale had ever been clocked on the surface. As the facts came in, flight planes were adjusted, navigational procedures corrected. Geared to the new meteorological conditions, the operation soon became routine, and the Japanese will finally collapsed in a blast of nuclear fire.

With peace this particular condition might have been forgotten or neglected. In the minds of many the explanation was a narrow one. The surprising velocity in the upper air blowing off northeast Asia was simply some sort of by-product of the seasonal monsoon winds. But to others, airmen and meteorologists alike, this glimpse of tremendous forces operating high aloft was stimulating, provocative and unforgettable.

While the commercial airlines waited for delivery of the new aircraft which would incorporate all the wartime advances in aeronautical design, their survey and weather planes kept poking their noses up to higher and higher levels. In the U. S. Weather Bureau, a new man from M.I.T. collated and studied all this information which was coming in from inside and outside his department. The result was curious, not to say astonishing. The air currents encountered high over Honshu proved to be no isolated phenomenon. Instead they apparently circled the globe about halfway between the equator and the pole, flowing from west to east to meet the sun.

The surprising thing about these early reports was not simply a confirmation of the high velocity of these winds, but that they seemed to be concentrated in the comparatively narrow width of a few hundred miles. They were therefore christened the *jet stream* and promptly became of intense interest to the whole world of aviation. For the new planes, as they came into service, were designed, like the Super-Fortresses, to fly at altitudes where the air's resistance is less than half that at the surface. In these postwar terms of high-flying reference, the difference between a head or tail wind of a hundred miles an hour was a matter of hard dollars and cents; indeed, a possibly essential factor in the safety and comfort by which Americans intended to maintain their aeronautical superiority.

This highly practical expectation, however, did not pay off. The jet stream was unfortunately found not to stay put. And as the British discovered, areas of extreme turbulence are suddenly encountered in clear skies without prior meteorological warning. Thus no national benefit was obtained from these first investigations. Indeed by one of those acts of international co-operation which seem to be going on all over the world without anybody paying much attention to them, the airlines of the principal nations got together and set up an overriding supranational authority. As a result of this convention, meteorological data, to guide the craft that fly the world's air routes, are now available from the surface up to the base of the stratosphere; in round figures, up to some fifty or sixty thousand feet.

III

Long before the war, meteorologists understood that certain atmospheric situations were reversed between the surface and the upper air. Where, for example, around the equator the air's pressure is low, aloft in the troposphere there is a level of high pressure. At the poles there is a similar reversal, but with high pressure at the ground and relatively low pressure up below the stratosphere. In between, along the horse latitudes, exists a band, shifting with the seasons, where the surface winds are weak or nonexistent. It is here—or at least slightly nearer the pole—that at forty or fifty thousand feet the upper air moves with its maximum velocity.

Based on the daily reports sent in by planes and weather ships which now supplement the older meteorological stations on land, the experts learned that the average position of the jet stream is situated over an area of surface calm. In general this swift and at times concentrated current marks the southern edge of a gigantic whirlpool. Below it, near the surface, a similar but smaller turntable of air swings around the North Pole. Thus one can imagine a gigantic inverted cone sitting on top of the world, its lower reaches spinning clockwise, its upper levels turning oppositely, from west to east.

In the southern half of the world we have little information to the south of Australia as to the movement of the upper air. But above this continent the edge of a similar vortex appears to be moving, likewise from west to east. In our hemisphere, these winds aloft increase steadily in speed from the pole down to somewhere short of the horse latitudes. Thereafter in both parts of the world they decrease in velocity, until close

103

to the equator they reverse their direction, to blow above the belt of the world weakly out of the east.

In most of nature's grand designs there is found a major over-all pattern, on which is superimposed a wealth of fine and often intricate detail. The first modification of this general behavior of the upper air is produced by the progress of the seasons. In winter the circumpolar vortex grows bigger, while the jet stream which marks its edge moves southward.

In this expansion the newly discovered current attains its highest velocity. Measured as high as two hundred miles an hour, it averages at this time of year some seventy or eighty. When the days lengthen into spring, the winds high aloft move more slowly, as the jet stream shifts back to the northward. By late summer its velocity drops to twenty-five or thirty miles an hour, as the whole polar cone in the atmosphere shrinks to its seasonal minimum.

The next detail in the design of the winds aloft is that produced by geography. Strongest where a cold continent stretches to the northeastward beside a warm ocean current close offshore, the jet stream seems to concentrate its strength where broad rivers of air at markedly different temperatures flow together below the stratosphere. Such a contrast between relatively hot and cold air would explain satisfactorily the areas of sudden turbulence encountered close to the stream's swift flow.

Such geographic conditions occur off the eastern United States and the Japanese Islands. High above the surface, these are two of the four locations where the jet stream attains its greatest velocity. Two other spots over the broad expanse of Russia mark additional centers of such maximum wind force, one above Moscow and another to the west of the Urals in Siberia. In summer, as the upper winds decrease in speed, these four centers move north, to become only three in number, one each to the south of the Icelandic and Aleutian lows, the third being consolidated out of the Russian two and coming to rest north of the summer center of low pressure in Central Asia.

Having acquired some knowledge of the seasonal behavior and of the geographic pattern of the jet current, the experts were startled to find a rhythm in its motion. This beat is being used tentatively—and to be sure with only moderate accuracy—to forecast the weather, not just from day to day but from week to week and even for a month at a time.

To predict the course of coming events one must be able to see in the present occurrence the form of the future fact. A scientist is of course much happier if he knows why something is happening, but in the early stages of new discovery he is more than satisfied if he can isolate some clear pattern in nature, whose basic form gives him assurance of an existing cause, albeit as yet unknown.

Our knowledge of the currents at the top of the troposphere is at present in this preliminary stage. The observed cycle in the jet stream runs over a period of four or five weeks. It begins most simply with the situation where this current flows from left to right across North America. Moving directly from west to east, it appears to imprison the cool, dry northern air, since at such times the United States is generally warmed by mild winds moving northward off the ocean.

Slowly at first the jet stream begins to undulate like a sluggish serpent. Below one or more of the deepening bulges which curve southward, a vast puddle of cold air moves down toward Texas or Florida. At the same time, within the coils that swing northward, the warm moist air moves into Canada. In about ten days or two weeks the jet stream's lateral flow is transformed into the shape of an enormous wave or double S, which lying on its side marks a path now traveling as great a distance north and south as it does east and west.

In another five or six days each loop bulging south begins

to close into a bag or sack. Within it the upper air whirls clockwise, while far below on the surface the heavy winds from the north sweep around in the same direction, carrying their cold strength southward. In between and far to the north the southern air will still remain in possession of the ground.

Such topsy-turvy conditions, of frost in Texas and thaw in Maine, are then ironed out by the development of a great frontal storm. Swirling from the surface counterclockwise up to those highest levels where the topmost currents are seeking to reestablish their direct flow from west to east, this final paroxysm will last about another week.

In this crescendo of wind and rain, the pressure originally built up over the pole is finally relieved; the atmospheric balance in the air's circulation is again restored. In a few days a high-flying weather plane, over Omaha or St. Louis, will report that the jet stream is once more flowing directly as a tail wind for any craft flying above twenty thousand feet from San Francisco to New York.

IV

Despite his towering skyscrapers and deepest gold mines, man in his movements is restricted essentially to two dimensions. The thin film within which he performs his vertical operations has been somewhat thickened by the advent of the aircraft, but the depth of this shallow shell is minute as compared to the distances he can travel across the length and breadth of his rounded planet.

Although this new instrument of war and commerce rises in the cosmic view but a comparatively infinitesimal distance above the earth's surface, yet the airplane operates by its nature in all three dimensions. To stay aloft it must move. And in its motions it must continually be aware of its height above the hard, unfriendly ground, as well as of its position relative to the world below it.

So long as an aircraft could travel only short distances, it proceeded best in a straight line above a lane marked out by surface landmarks. But once its range and ceiling were so increased that it could fly the featureless oceans, it had, like the old-time sailing ships, to seek for its benefit the best slant of wind. In these operations the moving currents of the atmosphere could become either an asset or a liability, a distinct help or a dangerous hindrance, with which long-range aviation found it was forced to deal.

To meet these postwar requirements, meteorology was asked to measure and chart, for the first time adequately and at frequent intervals of time, the air's movements within the whole depth of the troposphere. Given the money and facilities, the weather men found this naturally a big but nevertheless congenial task. Here in the upper air, they had good reason to believe, would be found many of the keys that would unlock new doors to greater meteorological knowledge.

To arrange this extensive array of information so as to determine the best route across the North Atlantic, from Gander, say, to Shannon, seemed to the first students of this aeronautical problem an almost superhuman job. Nevertheless it was done, more or less with a guess and a prayer, by long calculations giving the time in flight and the fuel needed for each one of the wide range of routes and altitudes. This labor was substantially reduced as a result of the close partnership which the war had first established and which peace was now cementing between aviation and meteorology. A leader in the older science had recognized how a well-known fact about the atmosphere could be given its proper aeronautical application.

Fortunately the air's changing pressure compels the winds to follow a corresponding pattern. In accordance therewith the air at any given level flows generally parallel to the contours marked out by the barometer. Although ridges and valleys intervene, the horizontal motion of the air is predominantly circular: clockwise in our hemisphere about a center of high pressure, the other way around about a focal point of low pressure.

In all its various formations, such alternations in the atmospheric pressure produce curving systems of winds which are geared together much like cogwheels or turntables, each in succession spinning oppositely to its neighbor. The answer supplied to the airmen was how to avoid bucking these curving currents, how to determine the route that rode them best. Given the pattern of the pressure, which the meteorologist supplies, not only are the winds predictable but the mathematics of dynamic flow reveal with a minor amount of calculation the best path to follow to reach a desired destination.

Since such a route will take the shortest time and require the least amount of fuel, it is in this sense the safest. But it is safer, too, for a further reason. The pattern which the air sets up by its curving movements separates widely the preferred route in one direction from that which is most desirable in the opposite way. One path will skirt one side of any atmospheric wheel; the other passes across the opposite side. Only where two such whirlpools mesh together will two oppositely flying aircraft be brought into proximity and have to establish different altitudes so as to pass each other safely.

By a comparatively quick and simple mathematical procedure the airlines now determine, for any given pattern of barometric pressure, the best route for any long-range flight. But they still require a series of charts of successive atmospheric levels, in order to select the most favorable pressure-pattern and hence the best altitude for their flight. Such charts are therefore prepared regularly for their use for heights above the ground increasing by some ten thousand feet at a time.

Such charts are proving to be of considerable help to the meteorologists themselves in making their daily forecasts. Prior to the war such predictions were based almost entirely on surface indications. Influenced by the different features of the earth's geography, the air close to the ground reacts to a large number of incidental factors which only in total relate to the weather's grand design. Above ten or twenty thousand feet, however, the meteorological picture is cleared of such minor details. Here reside the changes of pressure and temperature, which may on the one hand restrain, or on the other encourage, the development of the weather which is being felt and observed on the surface.

The movement of all our storms is guided or steered largely by the direction and force of the winds aloft. But the upper air also develops its own sweeps and rotations. If it is turning cyclonically, against the deflecting force, clouds will form and rain may fall, even though no frontal or other conditions are appearing close to the earth's surface to justify such worsening in the weather. When, in the reverse situation, the upper air is deflected by the force of coriolus into a clockwise spin in our hemisphere, the weather will be fine and clear, and any area of cloud or storm will have to travel around the edge of the resulting area of good weather.

The power and intensity of warm or cold front is likewise determined by movements of the air in these higher levels. For a cold front to be strong and violent, the surface winds must be blowing more vigorously into the frontal bulge than those in the upper layers of the atmosphere. Otherwise the winds aloft push the warm ascending air aside before it has a chance to be lifted rapidly by the cold air advancing along the ground far below.

The opposite situation encourages the formation of thick cloud and steady precipitation along the long slope of a warm front. Here the upper winds, blowing in the same direction as those nearer the earth, co-operate in thrusting out of the way the more powerful northern air. When the depths of the troposphere do not work together in this way, any warm front will be weak, its clouds thin, and little or no rain will fall.

In addition to its sideways motions as wind, the upper air sinks and rises. As the currents aloft swing and turn they at times come crowding together, while at others they sweep apart. Where on the one hand, in their whirls and eddies, these winds converge, the resulting build-up in pressure must be relieved, and so the air tends to move upwards. By such lifting to colder levels, clouds can be formed, entirely independently of any meteorological activity closer to the surface. Where, on the other hand, the upper currents are moving apart, the atmospheric pressure drops and the air above sinks down to redress the balance. In such a process of subsidence, any existing clouds move down into warmer levels and there tend to evaporate. And in general any movement earthward of the air aloft clears the sky and improves the weather.

When a winter thaw or summer heat wave moves up to us from the south, when a cold snap in late spring or cool air in early autumn comes down to us from Canada, each of these changes occurs on the surface only in co-operation with a corresponding action in the upper air. If the winds aloft are turning to their right, our weather far below will generally be clear. But if these currents are swinging the other way, they will produce the visible messengers of their progress, the high, lacy cirrus. The appearance of such clouds is evidence of the atmospheric adjustment which is taking place from the surface up to the base of the stratosphere and from which may be predicted increasing cloudiness and the likelihood of rain.

The picture of changing winds, shifting pressures and varying temperatures high above the earth has added largely to man's knowledge and understanding of the weather. But at the same time it has increased the scientific complexity of what he is required to explain. As usual in a case where new masses of data must be studied and assimilated, time will be required to work out the answers which describe the individual causes. So most likely we live today in the beginning of a new meteorological era as the vagaries of the jet stream are studied and the related patterns of the air's high currents are plotted for the planes that are flying greater and greater distances, faster and faster, at higher and higher altitudes.

Yet there is one simple point that emerges clearly. At times the whole depth of the troposphere moves and acts as a whole. At others the motion of the air close to the surface will be markedly different from that in the atmosphere's upper reaches. Such contrasts occur as some lower current thrusts under some upper layer, or when the winds aloft overrun the air stagnating closer to the ground.

Such contrasts as these may be gentle. Or they may be marked by an abrupt change in the air's temperature, in the force and direction of the wind or in the water vapor the atmosphere has in suspension. Close to the surface such differences between individual masses of air produce the frontal disturbances which are a prime feature of the weather in the middle latitudes. Aloft the horizontal surfaces along which such discontinuities exist are spots where the atmosphere may be storing its energy, building up its power. Largely absent from those geographic areas where good weather prevails as the air sinks steadily down from below the stratosphere, everywhere else from the tropics to the Arctic Circle such contrary conditions can be found taking shape between the upper and lower levels of the air.

In some cases such differences represent only the decay of past struggles, but in many others they hold the germ of new violence. Today meteorologists can identify a slight kink in the polar front and follow its development into a great storm.

111

No doubt as present knowledge expands, the weather fore-casters will learn enough to fix on some little discontinuity in the air aloft, recognizing it as the clue to a major shift of pressure in one of the troposphere's cells, by which the future weather may be predicted for days or weeks ahead.

CHAPTER VIII

What A Beautiful Belt, Said Alice

I

MODERN science, remembering the myths and superstitions which it first had to overthrow, condemns any sort of fantasy. All reasoning not based on observable fact is well considered to fall into this category. Therefore the serious geologists of the last century paid little attention to writers who discussed the question of the lost island of Atlantis, the characteristics common to the Aztec and early Egyptian cultures or the welcome given to the Spanish Conquistadors because the Indians believed that their white, bearded gods would return to them from across the western ocean.

There were indeed facts of a more solid nature to suggest a connection between the old world and the new. The arrangement of the rocks in western Europe and along the eastern seaboard of North America is strikingly similar. But this could be explained if both continents down the aeons of time had been molded by the same set of natural forces. Then too there were observations indicating that Greenland was moving away from Norway, although so slowly and imperceptibly that it was equally possible to assert the data was faulty.

Certainly without some facts explaining how the thing might have occurred, it was fantastic to consider that any land mass could have moved laterally across the surface of the earth. The discovery which gave this theory its initial measure of respectability came from a totally different science. Fantastically enough, it was in geodesy, whose job it is to determine the methods by which the continents may be mapped, that the means were found by which the exact position of Greenland and Norway is to be determined.

Unlike the schoolroom globe, the earth is not a perfect sphere. Flattened at the poles and even slightly out of round at the equator, its true shape is further obscured by the irregularities of its surface. If the position of any desired landmark is to be plotted with the extraordinary accuracy that modern instruments permit, the earth's basic outlines, independent of the oceans' depths or of the continents' mountains, must be included in the calculations.

Many of science's greatest disputes have raged over a frame of reference, have concerned a point of origin. The most famous is the one which brought Galileo before the Inquisition, by transferring the center of our solar system from the earth to the sun. Such is the problem of geodesy; to give the map makers an absolutely smooth, theoretic world to which all the real points above or below the mean level of the earth's oceans can be lowered or raised.

As this science first warmed to its task there seemed to be really no difficulty. If it be assumed that the interior of our planet consists of successive layers of first rock and then metal, each layer having the same weight or density, then variations in the force of gravity would tell the story of the world's essential departure from the truly spherical. Of course instruments of the most astonishing precision were necessary, but by the end of the last century these were available. As the results came in, they told quite a different tale.

There are two distinct ways of fixing the position of any terrestrial landmark. One is by astronomical observation, by finding the vertical angles that the heavenly bodies make at any location with the horizon. The other is by surveying, by measuring distances and horizontal angles from point to point across the earth's surface. When the topographical experts compared the results obtained by the two methods, they discovered, to the surprise of some, possibly to the annoyance of others, that the answers did not agree, that the two methods sometimes gave irreconcilable results. In most cases the differences were small, but here and there they proved to be substantial. A famous example is the one on the flat plain outside of Moscow, where the discrepancy is of the magnitude of a whole mile.

As the geodetists examined these figures and laid out new tests to greater degrees of accuracy, they were eventually forced to question a basis of reference immeasurably older than that which Galileo disproved. In all astronomical observations, the circle of the horizon is the plane above which the angle of any star is measured. This flat surface, as essential to the building of a temple as to the observation of a planet, had been established from the dawn of civilization by dropping to the ground a pointed weight attached to a length of string or cord. Down all the succeeding millennia, this direction, resulting from the pull of gravity, was assumed to point straight at the center of the earth. Perpendicular to this line lay the plane of the horizon.

With the growth of man's knowledge in modern times, he found that this age-old arrangement had to be corrected in one or both of two ways. First an allowance had to be made for any irregularities in the earth's surface, such as a hill or mountain whose gravitational mass might be pulling the plumb bob slightly sideways. A second correction was required for the amount by which the earth differed in shape from a perfect sphere.

As the nineteenth century drew to its close, a third factor was found to be preventing the plumb line from always pointting directly at the earth's center, and thereby to be causing

115

corresponding inaccuracies in the fixing of any geographical position by astronomical means. Modern spirit level or ancient plumb line was each being tilted out of the accurately horizontal or vertical, infinitesimally but definitely measurably, by gravitational differences which lay buried within the earth's crust.

The final conclusion—tested in every conceivable way down the past seventy-five years, since the result is revolutionary— was that the rock under the oceans is more massive than that which supports the land. To the geologists the discovery was of vital interest. The principle of *isostasy,* of a general balance in weight between an ocean area and an equivalent region of land, asserts that the continents ride high because they are light, that the seas' beds are depressed into basins because the rock beneath them is correspondingly heavy.

This conclusion does not mean that the balance is always perfect, that the land cannot rise or sink, down the span of geologic time, as the history of the sedimentary rocks asserts that it has. Instead it accounts for the fact, indicated by all geologic records, that what was now land has always been firmament and what had been originally sea was now as always covered by the ocean's depths.

To many of the men who had spent their scientific lives in cataloguing and comparing the earth's various strata, this theory did much more. At last they had a dynamic explanation of how the earth could change its contours, as the rain and snow slowly wore down the mountains and, scooping out the valleys, dumped the resulting debris out to sea along the coast. Like a summer iceberg melting slowly in the hot sun, such a reduction in weight would allow the continents to ride higher, as the slow process of erosion proceeded, year after geologic year. Or, and now the climatologists and meteorologists became interested, steadily thickening sheets of snow and ice, building up thousands of feet into the air, would cause the land below them to sink, exerting the whole pressure of this congealed water upon the earth's molten core.

Out of these adjustments and rearrangements of the world's weight, vast volcanic or other geologic disturbances might well have arisen. But a new and even more fundamental question now intruded. What was the reason for this distribution of dissimilar rock across the surface of the world? As the geodetists had initially assumed, a planet whose material had fallen together out of a gigantic blob of solar stuff should be nicely graded in weight from its massive center to its relatively lighter crust. What had stripped the top layer of granitic rock off more than half the earth, as an angry mother pulls the covers off a lazy child?

At its birth the world is assumed to have been incandescently hot, its rocks a viscous liquid like molten lava. Able to move as the new planet spun rapidly on its axis, they would have flowed toward the equator, giving the earth an outline much flatter through the poles than it has now that its crust has cooled. In its early orbit, it moved much closer each six months and then again much farther away from the parent sun than it does in its present yearly progress. A theory, somewhat too imaginative to win wide scientific endorsement, suggests that the moon was sucked or spun out of the earth's equatorial bulge at the time when the earth's crust was first beginning to harden.

A suggestion of this sort cannot be proved by direct observation, since the event is buried in time. Its scientific acceptance or disallowance can only come by the slow assemblage of often unrelated clues or unexpected data. Calculations do show that instability would be set up around the bulging waist of a spinning liquid ball as it became overlaid with a deepening, more solid crust. Thus this theory attempts to explain the rings of the planet Saturn, but indeed other explanations are equally possible.

In any event, the area from which the moon is presumed to have come is the Pacific Ocean. All around its vast area lies a chain of volcanoes, zones where the earth continually trembles and shakes, close to which are some of the deepest spots in all the oceans. For what the idea may be worth, this activity is considered the last remaining evidence of the departure of our satellite, of where went the covering rock upon which man stands, which has somehow disappeared from more than 60 per cent of the earth's surface.

II

Excluding the broad thumb of lower Africa, three land masses are all that appear in the southern hemisphere. Only a small fraction of the bottom half of the world is covered by the lighter rock on which the continents ride high. Except for South America, Australia, Antarctica and the bulge that ends at the Cape of Good Hope, all the rest is ocean, cradled by the heavier basalt that supports and balances the water's lighter weight.

Even the additional amount of land encompassed as one moves north to the Tropic of Cancer does not alter the fact that the weather of the tropics is born and bred primarily over the sea. Its effects upon the land are on the whole incidental to its oceanic origin. According to the broad picture of the general circulation of the atmosphere, moist maritime air is heated all around the waist of the world, lifting upwards toward the stratosphere. Below this resulting band of low pressure the surface winds die away. Toward this line of the doldrums, from the northeast and the southeast, moves the steady thrust of the trade winds.

In the dark days of 1942, civilian meteorologists in new naval uniforms found that this simple diagram of the air's tropical movements had substantially to be modified. The

Japanese possessed better knowledge and with the weather at their backs were moving relentlessly down the long chain of islands which ends with Australia. As each enemy task force steamed south behind a protective cold front, the weather men serving with our ships learned how deeply such thrusts of northern air can override the trade winds and push down into the main band of tropic weather.

One hundred years earlier there were plenty of American seamen who knew this area well. Their dusty logs and yellowed charts were helping the Navy's Hydrographic Office materially in supplying the necessary information for a war which few American naval officers had ever thought would come upon them so disastrously. But the whaling captains and their crews were resting quietly below the Seven Seas or in some peaceful New England graveyard, in New Bedford, Nantucket or perhaps the Vineyard. They could give no help to the meteorologists, since this science was not born when healthy, handsome Polynesians were being taught the old songs and chanteys to the accompaniment of the seaman's guitar, an instrument of a wide range of sizes, strung against the damp sea air with strings of steel.

So, against a background of defeat and disillusion, a war began which was to be fought on the sea and from island to island and in the air off the tiny dot of a carrier's deck. In these operations the mythologists, in Admiral Halsey's wry designation, found that forecasting the tropical weather was something entirely different from the problems to which they were accustomed, in the higher latitudes where they had learned their trade.

III

From Guayaquil in Ecuador due west to Singapore is half the circumference of the earth, which here runs some eleven thousand nautical miles across the Pacific Ocean. To the north and south there are spinning two whirlpools of circling winds, at whose centers the air descends slowly from the top of the troposphere. These two vast vortices can be imagined as if they were geared together, the teeth of their cogs meeting along the equator. Here their motion is from the east, from the sunrise toward the west, where the sun sets.

Since the air's gases are not rigid but compressible, the currents begin to crowd together where they blow down from the northeast and up from the southeast. Before passing between the two centers of high pressure, the atmosphere rises strongly towards the stratosphere, the daily heat of the sun assisting the crowding air streams to lift upwards as they move at the same time toward Asia. Here where the air is urged aloft by the force of both the horizontal and the vertical circulation, towering cumulus clouds build up as the sun mounts higher in the heavens. From these in mid afternoon may come the sudden showers typical of such parts of the tropical oceans.

Yet further westward a contrary meteorological situation exists. Beyond the spot where the two atmospheric wheels may be imagined to be enmeshed, the winds are relieved from their previous crowding. Here their currents start diverging, spreading out as if along the curved spokes of a vast fan. Reacting to the drop in pressure produced by this divergence, the drier air aloft sinks down and reduces the high humidity of the surface layers. Such subsidence is working against the heat of the sun as it warms and tries to lift the surface air upwards.

Along the tropics the islands that lie beneath areas of generally subsiding air enjoy the pleasantest weather. Hawaii below the North Pacific high is such a chosen meteorological spot. But far to the south, lying on the equator, is the tiny dot of Christmas Island. Although surrounded by immense stretches of water, its rainfall is so scanty that it is practically devoid of vegetation.

Such islands—and they are not uncommon in the Pacific—hardly fit the conventional picture of lush foliage glistening in the rain of heavy tropical showers. In many other ways the weather over the equatorial oceans varies from spot to spot, changing, too, with the progress of the seasons. For example, the pair of atmospheric whirlpools which generate a large part of the tropical weather are only of equal power and extent for a brief period in spring and autumn. Even then one is expanding as its half of the world warms up, while the other is contracting as cold darkness settles on the opposite pole.

In general the surface winds are imagined as moving from the horse latitudes diagonally toward the equator where the air is pictured as rising vertically to flow north and south below the base of the stratosphere. Around the equatorial band of ascending air are situated the calms of the doldrums. This trough of low pressure moves with the seasons and in moving materially changes its nature.

As it shifts, say, north in April and May, the corresponding vortex above it is growing greater, the one to the south less powerful. In that half of the world where winter is settling over Antarctica, the circular sweep of the air is changing into the generally straighter thrust of the trade winds, blowing more and more steadily from the southeast. Thus the North Pacific high no longer wheels in gear with a southern companion, but rather against a line of parallel air currents. Where around the perimeter of this growing circle the winds curve down from the north, they meet their southern cousins in a narrow elongated band. Here the air often ascends violently, forming a long wall of towering cumulus clouds. These can be marked by fierce thunderstorms out of whose tops and sides altostratus and cirrus rise in successive layers to fifty or sixty thousand feet.

121

Stretching from east to west in a continuous line of squalls and waterspouts, such an intense equatorial front is a major hazard to aircraft flying north or south across the equator. Indeed the nature of this meteorological phenomenon became fully understood only with the development of modern aviation. Its violence, however, is seldom long-lasting. Having risen to its crescendo, in two or three days it will fade away, until only a long line of billowing, congested or fair-weather cumulus remains to mark the paroxysm.

IV

Of all the manifestations of the world's weather, the terrible tropical hurricane is undoubtedly the best known and the most feared. The name comes from the Carib Indians' word for a big wind. Called typhoons in the northwestern Pacific, cyclones over the Indian Ocean and Willi-willies where they strike Australia, these great whirling storms sweep out a path of concentrated destruction. Spawned over the vast reaches of the empty sea, they reach their maximum intensity only in the western portions of the oceans.

Originating about ten degrees north or south of the equator, they then move westward around one or other of the oceanic high pressure areas, to sweep northward against the Philippines or off the coast of North America, southward upon Australia. Except for those few which move inland and lose their strength over the land, they then curve back toward the eastward between latitudes twenty and thirty. Here, over the cooler waters, they slowly dissipate their enormous power.

At times, however, as in 1938 and again six years later, such a storm does not recurve back out to sea. Held to a northerly path by some extreme westward position of the Bermuda high, it strikes the New England coast, bringing into the middle latitudes the same devastation that annually threatens the islands of the Caribbean.

Across a width of some hundred miles gale winds blow and torrential rains fall. Over an area whose diameter is five to ten times this, the pressure of the storm is felt. Its destructive power is produced by an assemblage of complementary meteorological actions, nicely arranged to bring maximum devastation to low-lying island and tropical coast line.

It is not simply the power of the wind which may average as high as 120 miles an hour. At the same time the air is fiercely turbulent; individual gusts strike houses and trees and other obstructions with a velocity that may be twice the average. As the storm moves forward, the winds change direction, quickly and sharply near the center, more slowly and less radically farther out. Weakened by the first assault on one side, such objects fall more easily before an attack from a new direction.

This disturbance to the air is evidence of the enormous suction pulling the atmospheric gases inwards and thence upwards. Indeed a hurricane is the largest and grandest meteorological machine in existence for turning water vapor into cloud and rain. Within such storms the barometer drops to its lowest known readings. Relieved of this part of the atmosphere's weight, the tides along the seacoast often rise to unprecedented levels. In narrow or shallow waters, particularly when the winds blow toward the shore, the sea floods inland like a tidal wave.

In 1938, and again in 1944, much of the damage along Long Island and the New England coast was caused in this way. Many who observed the aftermath of the first storm will always remember the hero of the classic story which appeared shortly afterwards in *The New Yorker*. He had bought a new barometer. When it was delivered and unpacked, it stood stubbornly, no matter how severely tapped, well below "stormy." Angrily he repacked the defective instrument and drove back with it to the express office. When he returned home, nursing his ill temper and noting the steady worsening of the weather, he found his house had been blown into Great South Bay.

All meteorological moods of violence are formed from contrast and difference. But before the development of long-range aircraft, little was known about tropical or equatorial weather that was contrasting or different. Now, out of the war's experience and continuing postwar investigation, appreciation is growing that the disturbance from which a hurricane can form is a comparatively common occurrence within the tropics. The air along the equator is not all hot and humid, its movement is not simply a steady lifting toward the base of the stratosphere.

In general the progress of equatorial weather moves with the rising sun, from east to west. Differing markedly from the rhythm to north and south, it has its own changes that on an annual scale produce its familiar alternation of dry and rainy seasons. On the shorter basis of day to day and week to week, the generally light, easterly winds move in beats, their velocity rising to freshness or falling to dead calm as they blow weakly westward. The center of such atmospheric waves is found high above the surface, at ten or twenty thousand feet. Their progress has been marked from the eastern shores of the great oceans, so they must initially form over the land.

Centered high overhead, these beats are no doubt part of the adjustments by which the atmosphere in one place is continually redressing the unbalance constantly being re-established somewhere else. Such a bulge of originally continental air slopes back eastward aloft, the air on the surface spreading out to bring fair weather ahead of it. To its rear the currents crowd together, so that its passage westward is followed by cloudiness and showers.

124

Within these shifting airs quite commonly form the initial depression, the minor cyclonic swirl, which can expand into a major hurricane. Such full-scale development, however, is comparatively rare. The equatorial air is fanning out as it approaches the opposite coast, such divergence tending to clear the skies and fill up any atmospheric area of low pressure. Off the land to the westward must come the contrast out of which such a storm can occasionally grow.

Over all the western portions of the tropical oceans, the winds aloft blow down towards the equator out of the west. Much drier than the lower, moisture-laden easterlies, they are usually warmer as well. Descending as they do from below the horse latitudes, this air is initially about the warmest and driest in the world. To indicate its source at the top of the troposphere, it is called *superior air* and occasionally in mid-summer such air comes down upon the surface over the high mountains and tablelands of our southwestern states.

Its warmth forms the well-known trade wind inversion which in winter holds down the tops of the fair weather cumulus to about ten thousand feet. In summer it rises to twenty or thirty thousand feet, beneath which the congested cumulus rise towering in the rainy season. In the in-between times of spring and autumn, a tongue of such dry northern air may thrust down towards the equator, overriding and pressing down with unusual force on some small cyclonic depression taking shape to the eastward of the Caribbean.

If within this upper mass the currents become twisted, to turn in the same direction as those on the surface, a hole may be punched in this continental air aloft, an atmospheric vortex form, by which the wet air close to the surface can spin rapidly up to the condensation level. Held down by the inversion above them, the surface winds move circling toward the point of their release upward.

Flying far out to sea in the hurricane's season, weather

125

planes now search for such a storm's beginnings. When found, it is named for some wife or sweetheart. Thereafter, as Mary, Agnes or Dorothy grows from innocent girlhood, her track is carefully plotted so that her future course may be predicted; her development closely followed so that her mature charms may be effectively estimated.

Moving generally at twenty to twenty-five miles a day, such a storm, however, can act as unpredictably as does the favored lady for whom it was named. At times they slow to a halt; at others suddenly hasten forwards. Generally following their curving track, they may veer off without a moment's notice and come straight in toward the land.

Tracking the hurricane is a dangerous occupation. Out of it has come a better understanding of the forces and conditions in which those atmospheric whirlpools are born and bred. To all except the specialists the best thing to do is to fly, sail or steam away from its center and out of its path. This is hardest to do when a craft is situated between the hurricane and the neighboring maritime high-pressure sea. In our hemisphere, this is what seamen term the dangerous northern half.

All sectors, however, are dangerous, since to get out of the region of wind and storm most directly, one should steam in the trough of the mounting seas. Facing the wind the center is to your right in the northern half of the world and a little astern. Riding close-hauled on the proper tack, with a handkerchief of sail, was the expedient of the old-time sailing ship.

Things are easier today, for all ships and planes that can move out of its expected path. But on the islands that may lie across its path, there is still no defense against the hurricane except the heaviness of the houses' walls and the stoutness of the trees' roots.

CHAPTER IX

Bring Out The Chart

I

A THEORY of art, one might well think, has little place in the story of a science. Yet scientists often declare they derive deep aesthetic satisfaction from their chosen fields. In many such instances the levels at which scientific beauty resides are so lofty that they are well out of reach of the uninitiated, but in other cases the average man is able to share the scientist's pleasure without having to acquire much or any of his background knowledge or erudition.

Cartography is an excellent case in point. The science of map making depends on some fairly advanced mathematics, but well-made charts and maps are, of their very nature, attractive, fascinating things to a wide variety of people. On the scientific side the problem is how to represent, for the purpose intended, a portion of a sphere on a flat piece of paper. Once, however, the most desirable projection is devised or determined, the map maker is primarily concerned with two questions which have distinctly aesthetic implications.

In the first place the making of a map, like the making of a model, is concerned with reducing the size of an assemblage of objects. But, unlike a model, a map generally requires such a large reduction in scale that all details cannot possibly be reproduced. For example, the maker of a model engine may duplicate each individual bolt and rivet, whereas the cartog-

127

rapher must be content to depict the woods, since he cannot possibly indicate each individual tree.

The map maker's second problem is how best to represent all the various details that he does want to show, to the reduced scale that makes his map the useful, convenient thing he wants it to be. For this purpose he uses symbols. They are technically called *conventional signs,* according to which, for example, a village may be a dot; a town, a small circle; and a capital, a star.

In his graphic arts, man seems to feel that the representation must never be purely realistic or simply photographic. Some objects must be emphasized, others suppressed; certain things should be exaggerated, others minimized. Perhaps it is that the human eye enjoys being fooled, or perhaps the artist must attempt to duplicate the selective process by which the mind scans the visual scene. In any event, aesthetic satisfaction clearly arises from the artist's solution by choice of a problem with which the map maker must deal out of necessity.

The cartographer is likewise forced to employ symbols, for the thoroughly practical purpose of representing to his comparatively tiny scale the geographic or other features which he wishes to reproduce. In the development of visual art, a different kind of symbolism has often taken shape as a sort of artistic shorthand. In most old or long-established civilizations many details are found assuming a more and more conventional shape, by which they come to suggest rather than depict the objects they purport to picture.

Historically the growth of symbolism has generally marked the decay of artistic vigor. Yet presumably the viewer of such art enjoyed the act by which his imagination projected a few blobs and squiggles into pomegranate or palm tree. The conventional signs of cartography are, to be sure, primarily utilitarian in purpose, but they may also stimulate the mind's eye to imagine mountains and oceans, busy cities and empty, waterless deserts.

Modern maps and charts are made for a wide variety of purposes. Fifty years ago railroad maps were the exciting things at vacation time that automobile maps are today. Both are designed to emphasize these two respective methods of transportation. The maps of a schoolboy's Geography on the other hand serve a more general end; they are designed to represent the various features of the earth's surface: oceans and continents, rivers and bays, lakes and islands, mountains and deserts.

For more technical uses there are produced geologic, topographic, military, nautical and oceanographic maps, charts or surveys. But in every piece of cartography certain details must be left out for lack of space and interest, while at the same time many of those features which do appear must be exaggerated in size or scale in order to bring out the data each map is intended to depict. Superimposed on such exaggeration are the shorthand symbols by which the map maker represents a lighthouse or a mine, an airport or a swamp.

On the practical side this is the essence of the making of a map. But it is the way the cartographer selects his method of emphasis, designs his conventional signs and applies the colors which will distinguish and illuminate his boundaries that in total determines the aesthetic pleasure that the finished work will supply.

II

In the history of cartography, maps for some particular purpose usually are produced first in a crude, utilitarian shape. Then as many hands work over them, their form and details become objects of increasing care and attention. In time they then grow more and more aesthetically appealing to the eye and to the imagination. Weather maps in the past fifty years have passed through this development until today with their curving fronts, their sweeping isobars, the figures and symbols surrounding each reporting station, they are things of considerable beauty.

Not so long ago, before the Scandinavian theory of conflicting air masses was fully understood and accepted in the United States, the main basis for forecasting our weather was the distribution and alteration in the pressure of the atmosphere. A weather chart in those days consisted principally of an assemblage of curving lines, no one of which crossed any of its neighbors. Each such isobar—*iso* stemming from the Greek word meaning equal—records the points along which the height of the barometer is the same.

On a topographical map a single contour line runs through a series of points all at the same level above sea level. Even to the unskilled eye these sweeping lines depict the shape of the undulating country: steepest where the contours crowd together, flattening into gentler slopes as they spread apart. Unlike the stable earth, however, the atmosphere's pressure is continually shifting and changing above our heads, so that a weather map is made up for a particular instant of time. But for that instant the sweeping isobars depict in the moving air much that is comparable to what the contours reveal for the solid earth.

As symbols, the isobars offer the first challenge to the imagination. As they curve and swing, the mind's eye can picture the air adjusting itself to the mysterious strains and stresses imposed upon it as it moves throughout its height above the surface of the earth. Where these lines of equal pressure crowd close together, the atmospheric adjustments will be marked by high winds and other forms of meteorological violence. Where they are spaced far apart, the air

130

becomes still and gentle, the skies either clear or evenly overcast.

Where a contour encloses a rough circle of emptiness, there on a topographical map is marked the summit of a hill or mountain. Similarly a closed isobar, enclosing the letter H or L, tells where an area of high or low pressure has its center. Around this the mind's eye can picture the winds swinging in their proper clockwise or counterclockwise sweep, while at the same time it may imagine the air sinking slowly down and out or rising more strongly upward and inward.

This trick of comparing the isobars with the older idea of contour lines has produced a phraseology in the meteorological fraternity by which the shifting barometric pressure is described in terms of physical ups and downs. A high pressure area is called a *high*, while its opposite, as well as being known as a *low*, is alternately described as a *depression*.

This visualization of the air's pressure or the mercury's height is carried over into those cases where two adjacent highs are separated by a band of low pressure or where two neighboring depressions are held apart by an area where the barometer is comparatively higher. The first corresponds to a valley between two hills and is called a *trough*, while its opposite is similar to a mountain range and is termed a *ridge*.

These are of course not simply technical terms. They represent how man, incurably attached to the workings of his imagination, has translated into picturesque language the new things that his scientific probings have developed. As the meteorologist on duty assigns to some storm center the name of a favored girl, the amateur can, if he wishes, well remember that no science is the dry-as-dust subject that it may appear from its outer and often complicated surface.

III

The barometer is an excellent means of forecasting the immediate weather. But its movements, although they closely measure, do not help much to explain the meteorological phenomena of our middle latitudes. The theory that probably did most to clarify such changes was enunciated in Norway during the first world war. Here the talented son of a distinguished father set forth his first ideas which in time were to become a foundation stone of modern meteorology.

The contribution of Bjerknes was to consider the dynamic properties of conflicting air masses, of atmospheric parcels at different temperatures, possessing different humidities and moving in different directions. The surface where two such different blobs of air are in direct contact is called a *front*. Curving sharply or sloping gently high into the atmosphere, this boundary where two opposing masses of air are in opposition appears on the weather map as a thick line, showing the position of the front where it rests on the surface of the earth.

Probably no other single idea has contributed so much to making the weather's progress graphically interesting as this theory of differing masses of air and of their conflict along a frontal zone. On a weather map the properties of each air mass are indicated by figures and symbols placed about each reporting station, while the development of the frontal struggle is marked by the type of front reported. These are of four types: *warm, cold, stationary* and *occluded.*

A *cold front* is where the forces of the north are pushing forward violently to victory and is represented by a series of spikes pointing in the direction in which the front is advancing. A *warm front,* on the other hand, is the line where the long ramp up which the southern air is flowing rests on the earth's surface. It is symbolized by a succession of solid half circles, also on the side in which the front is moving.

132

Where a stalemate has occurred, where one sort of front or the other has come to a halt, the result, often only a temporary one, is a *stationary front*. On a weather chart this is shown by alternate spikes and circles, each symbol placed on the side corresponding to the type of air it depicts.

An *occluded front* occurs in the mature stages of a cyclonic storm, when a cold front has swept around and overtaken the warm front ahead of it. Generally the more powerful cold air, like a rooting pig, lifts the warmer southern winds. As a result there are in existence two fronts, one above the other: on the ground an advancing cold front, aloft a slower-moving warm front expending its last energies in the storm's crescendo. On the weather map such a frontal line shows the same alternation of spikes and circles as for a stationary front, but since an occluded front is moving across the surface of the earth, both sets of symbols are on the same side of the line, pointing in the direction of motion.

With its spaced isobars, with its thicker lines symbolizing the existing frontal systems, a meteorological map conveys to the weather-wise a picture of moving air streams, of forming clouds and of growth or decay in any area of storm and rain. Within such a picture are framed many of the clues to the future, as to how the weather will develop or progress. But first there is considerably more that such a chart finds space to express.

The nature of any frontal conflict is largely determined by the properties of the air masses which are locked in combat. Such differences arise as air is warmed or chilled over some particular region of origin. On the map the characteristics of each mass of air is noted by two initials. The first is either c or m; written, that is, in lower case. These report whether the air was bred over land or water: c for continental, m for maritime.

The second letter, written as a capital, states in what part of the globe the air mass originated: A for Arctic, P if above the polar front, T if below the tropics, and E when it comes from close along the equator. In the United States we receive no equatorial air nor much if any continental tropical due to the narrowing land to the south of us. We do, however, have occasional incursions of a meteorological maverick. This is air that descends in summer over the mountains of the southwest directly from below the stratosphere. Its initial is S for *superior air*. It is the driest and, by the time it reaches the surface, generally the hottest sort of air that can be found on earth.

In the United States the maximum degree of conflict occurs when dry, cold polar or arctic air meets warm, wet maritime tropical. A less violent clash takes place when air moving southeastward out of the northern Pacific collides with that ranging up from the Gulf of Mexico. The maritime air from the North Pacific starts off fairly cold and wringing wet. But in its passage over the Rocky Mountains most of its water vapor is turned into rain, so that it descends into the Middle West warm and dry. Its temperature, therefore, is not much different from that of its Atlantic cousin. What contrast there is, is due to the difference in moisture content.

Yet, although each great puddle of air can thus be conveniently labeled, each has its own individual characteristics, which in turn are variously modified as it moves out and away from the region where it was first born and bred. A sampling of these properties is made at each weather station. These, together with the additional symbols which describe the state of the weather, comprise the main features of a weather map. But no such chart is actually a thing by itself; each is just one synoptic recording of a sequence of events moving in space and time. Day by day, a succession of weather maps record the continuing, never-ending story of what is occurring in the sky above us. Often the next development is as predictable as the outcome of a familiar tale, but at times it is as unexpected as a child's shattering remark to an adult company.

IV

A weather map is somewhat like the usual photograph taken with the ordinary camera. It records the meteorological situation at a given instant; at the very moment, that is, when the shutter is snapped. Instead of this still picture, man may someday devise a means of making a movie of the changing data which comprise our weather. Until that time, however, our imaginations must supply the active factor to what is at present a static portrayal.

For this purpose a knowledge of the direction and velocity of the wind is an essential third element to the sweeping isobars and the curving fronts. Therefore on each weather station an arrow is located whose barb is replaced by the circle which on a geographic map often denotes a town or city. Unlike that on a weather vane, each arrow is directed as if flying with the wind, its circular head pointing in the direction toward which the wind is blowing.

On this symbol the number of feathers indicates the wind's force. They are placed for simplicity all on one side of the shaft. Three full lines, for example, indicate a wind blowing between 25 and 31 miles an hour, while six is the maximum and represents a gale of 75 miles an hour or greater. For the range of speeds between a dead calm and the force of a gale, the number of feathers and half-feathers denote, to a scale devised by a British admiral, how fast the wind is blowing. Called the Beaufort scale, it is more sensitive to light airs than to strong winds. It is here printed on the End Papers, where it can be consulted as one's knowledge and interest expand.

For the use of airmen, weather maps are produced, for a

135

succession of altitudes, depicting the weather aloft. At heights above three or four thousand feet, the winds blow closely parallel to the isobars. At ground level, however, friction slows up and deflects them so that here the moving air often blows diagonally outward from a high, inward towards a low. Hills and mountain ranges, large lakes or neighboring oceans can likewise distort, close to the earth's surface, the basic relation between the air's movement and the atmospheric pressure.

So in examining each weather map, one must be prepared for the occasional appearance of discrepancies between the isobaric pattern and the arrows denoting the wind's direction and velocity. Such vagaries or contradictions are part of the weather's imponderable nature and on a lesser scale appear at all altitudes. In fact, despite all our increasing meteorological knowledge the weather still retains the charm of the uncertain, the inconstant and at times the unpredictable.

V

Just as the symbols for the direction and force of the winds illuminate the pattern of the isobars, so the temperature at each recording station helps dramatize the clashing masses of opposing air. Across a strong cold front, for example, a difference of twenty or thirty degrees may be recorded, while one that is losing its power will show little drop in temperature from one side to the other. Or, when polar air is pushing down the Mississippi while at the same time warm winds from the Caribbean are ranging up the eastern seaboard, it can be colder in Texas than it is in Maine.

On some of the maps printed in the daily papers the figures for the temperature and the symbols for the force and direction of the wind are the only two items which are reproduced out of the much more extensive data on the master map. By symbols or numerals this information goes on to include the

nature of the high, low and middle clouds, the past and present
state of the weather, the visibility and ceiling, the atmospheric
pressure and its trend over the previous three hours, the
amount of recent precipitation and the air's humidity.

Much of this mass of data is provided for the use of flyers.
The airplane has not only been an important means of expanding our knowledge of the weather's behavior, but at the
same time it has made its own demands for additional information not previously required by sailors, farmers and the
older, ground-rooted professions. In addition to wishing to
know all about the winds and weather aloft, the aviator is
deeply concerned with the fog, haze or precipitation which
may make it dangerous or impossible for him to land his
aircraft. The height of the lowest clouds is also of crucial
importance as he approaches his destination, while icing and
thunderstorms are hazards in his straight and level flight.

Spurred by the progress of aviation, meteorology's conventional signs have become internationally standardized, and
these symbols, together with the necessary supporting figures,
are now arranged in a uniform pattern around each station,
ship or aircraft whose report is included on the map. Each type
of cloud has its own shorthand mark. Another set describes
the state of the weather: if fair, the degree of cloudiness and
any factors affecting the visibility; if stormy, the type and
intensity of the rain, snow or other precipitation.

Imaginative and suggestive as these symbols are, informa-
tive too as the figures which go with them, in total they are
much too unwieldy for general reproduction. A map for the
use of the average man, therefore, will show simply by cross-
hatching where precipitation has fallen in the past twelve hours.
Elsewhere the weather must be constructed imaginatively from
the sweep of the isobars and by the lines of the fronts. Yet as
the clouds roll up over the horizon or clear away to a cloud-
less sky, the amateur may become dissatisfied with his lack of

137

meteorological information, with the broad statements of the weather reports, and may well wish for increasing data on the subtler shades of the weather's drama. Played on a global scale, its characters act out their never-ending roles for an audience for whom the only price of admission is to look upward with a little knowledge and attention.

VI

During the morning of April 3, 1952, a small center of low pressure was situated over Western Texas. Out towards the Gulf of Mexico a long cold front, extending eastward across southern Florida and out into the Atlantic, had come largely to a halt. To the north a simple circular depression was bringing rain to the Great Lakes, while westward cold, dry air out of Canada was moving down across the border. Beyond the Rockies a second center of high pressure was moving into Oregon.

When the weather map was made up at 1:30 P.M., the little cell of low pressure in the southwest was developing a minor frontal line of its own and had hitched itself up at right angles to the almost stationary cold front. From this point of attachment out to the coast, the old front was beginning to move back northward as a warm front, in response to the air flowing upwards between the old high over Georgia and the young depression developing to the west.

The chart made up at lunchtime today is the one that makes tomorrow's morning newspapers. To the reader riding to work on April 4th, the wind arrows and the station temperatures told a story of sharply contrasting air: one stream flowing cold and assuredly dry out of the northwest, the other warm and presumably wet, off the Gulf up the lower Mississippi. The winds, he would have noted, were blowing gently between widely spaced isobars, but with some rain beginning to fall in Kansas and Texas the condensing water vapor could act quickly to tighten these lines of equal atmospheric pressure.

In the spring of the year there is little difference in the southern states between the temperature of land and ocean. In Canada, however, winter still holds much of its dominion. Thus in mid-March or early April extreme contrasts in the thermometer's reading can develop from north to south down the great plain stretching from the Arctic Sea to the Gulf of Mexico. On the map of April third the temperature at Galveston was seventy, at Winnipeg twenty-seven. Out of such differences can grow our great spring storms.

On this day the weather man with his charts of the winds high aloft could mark the southward surge of the jet stream, within whose resulting bulge such storms expend their full violence. But the man in the street had only the surface map. Yet this suggested clearly what might be expected. The two highs to the north and northwest would urge eastward the growing area of low pressure in the southwest, while the air sweeping around between the old high in Georgia and the circular low over the Lakes could lead it up the valleys of the Mississippi and the Ohio.

Weather maps are plotted every six hours and take about two hours to prepare and transmit. Four maps later, as of 1:30 P.M. on April 4th, the young storm, now a healthy disturbance, had become the dominant feature of the chart. Moving northeasterly, it was bringing rain to a wide area reaching from New Orleans north to Chicago and eastward to Buffalo. Around its center the increasing winds and closer spacing of the isobars testified to the decreasing pressure that was arising with this condensation and precipitation. Ahead of it, along the coast, warm cloudy winds from the Atlantic were blowing inland to meet in New England the colder air being left behind as the old circular depression moved onward above the St. Lawrence.

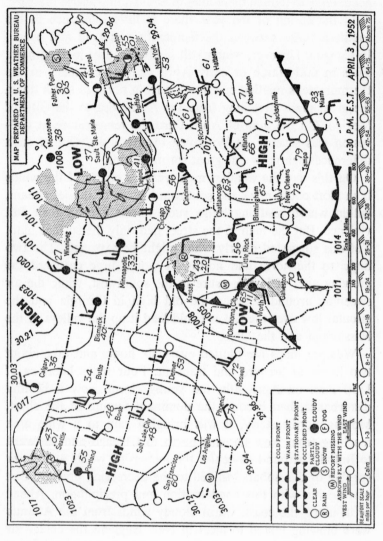

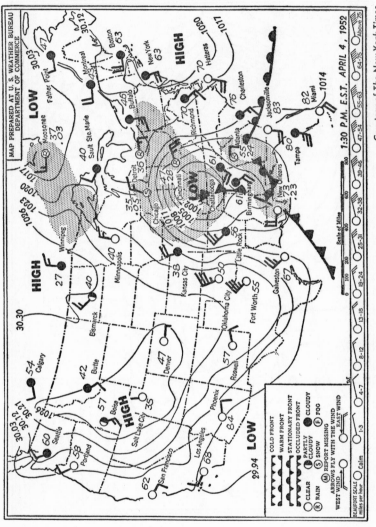

MAP PREPARED AT U. S. WEATHER BUREAU
DEPARTMENT OF COMMERCE

1:30 P.M. E.S.T. APRIL 4, 1952

Courtesy of The New York Times

141

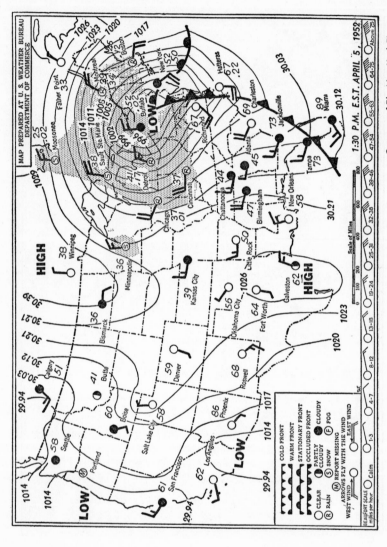

Courtesy of The New York Times

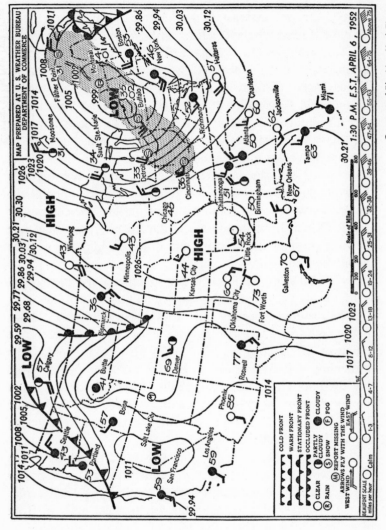

This strong contrast ahead of the storm's probable line of progress indicated the likelihood of its continuing growth. A householder at breakfast in any northeastern city on April 5th did not need the paper's forecast to get the story. Centered now somewhere south of Lake Erie, the storm was still growing in intensity, its effects clearly visible outside his window. His newspaper did, however, contain a meteorological story of violence and destruction in which six people had been killed, over fifty injured and many hundreds made homeless. Wiping out one town completely, tornadoes had slashed a path of devastation across four southern states.

On April 3rd, the weather map had featured two highs in the west: the one over Canada formed of cold, continental air; the one above Oregon coming down from the warmer, wetter Pacific Ocean. In its progress over the Rockies, such maritime air loses most of its moisture and descends into the western plains dry and clear.

As the little low in Texas began to expand and move eastward, the map of the next day showed that the colder Canadian high had shifted its center only a little way southward. Down to Kansas City, where the temperature was 38°, it had thrust a tongue of its cold air. But below this point, behind the deepening depression, the originally maritime winds were flowing into Oklahoma and Texas. Blowing strongly in a narrow current, as the wind arrows showed, they had come from one ocean to another and at Galveston were entering the Gulf of Mexico.

Over Arkansas, however, this stream was turning to its left, flowing eastward into the southern sector of the low pressure area. Warmed as it moved south, it was still cooler by ten or fifteen degrees than the wet tropical mass in front of it. Far ahead of where the line of frontal contact rested on the surface, the impetus of the western winds was carrying them forward aloft. Overrunning the moist, hot flow from the

144

Gulf, the dry cool air bulged, as the day progressed, further and further toward the east.

At an altitude of only a few thousand feet, a sharp, unstable contrast was developing over southern Louisiana and Mississippi. Above this level the air was dry and cool aloft; below it, warm and wet. As the sun rose higher on April 4th, the air at the surface became steadily hotter, its own natural instability growing greater as the temperature mounted.

Under these circumstances the first errant current that could ascend vertically and pierce this upper layer of discontinuity would then enter new and cooler levels, where its further ascent would be immediately and violently encouraged. Such a rapid, whirling climb would suck the wet air nearer the surface into a twisting funnel of angry destruction. Such is the southwestern tornado.

These conditions are well understood meteorologically, their occurrence comparatively easy to predict. But what the forecaster is totally unable to foretell is where any individual tornado will form or strike. The area of danger will generally cover hundreds or thousands of square miles, while the path of each twister may be only a few hundred yards wide, its course entirely erratic and uncertain. Like its close cousin, the waterspout, it is the most concentrated and eccentric of all the weather's many manifestations.

With the midday map of April 5th, the storm had about reached its maximum intensity. All across the northeast, reaching back to Detroit and Chicago, rain or snow was falling. In the shape of an inverted pear, cyclonic winds blew between crowded isobars whose center was now located near Buffalo. Paralleling the eastern seaboard, its attendant cold front draped its length a thousand miles southward. To the west, close to the storm's original breeding place, the Pacific high was entering the Gulf of Mexico, while far to the north

145

the cold Canadian air mass still stood seemingly irresolute above the border.

When in its final stages the storm at last moved out to sea, this fair weather from the west would advance into the eastern states. But whether it would hasten or retard the spring, whether it would be cool or warm, that would depend on which of the two western highs achieved the stronger circulation. Another act in the ever-changing meteorological drama was being set on the weather's stage.

CHAPTER X

What Of The Night?

I

THIS is an age of science; America is a scientific country. And yet our scientific achievements have been curiously one-sided; in one important respect our science has been severely limited. Admiring predominantly the practical, seeking primarily the achievement of useful results, the first settlers of the United States seem to have handed down to the latest citizens a deep-rooted suspicion, indeed a working hostility, for the purely theoretical.

In those few cases where Americans have made basic additions to scientific theory, their work was largely neglected at home. What appreciation they did receive, came in the main from their foreign colleagues. Our forte has been to erect a shiningly efficient superstructure, on theoretical foundations laid by others. The fundamental reasoning that led to the development of the Atom Bomb, for example, was largely performed by European expatriates. Except in one or two cases the American contribution was in overcoming essentially practical problems of a theoretically secondary nature.

The enthusiasm with which Americans eventually accept a new idea should not blind us to the considerable lag in time which generally occurs before we become even aware of its existence. Einstein's first theories began issuing from Zurich at the turn of the century, but the American public was not much interested in the resulting revolution in scientific think-ing until some twenty years later. The ideas of Bjerknes had been pretty well formulated for a decade and a half before the first frontal line appeared on a U. S. Weather Map.

There are currently signs and indications that American thinking in terms of the relation between theory and practice is beginning to change. Thrust more or less unwillingly to the front in world affairs, the people of the United States are faced with a number of unpleasant human chores. They are finding that they must separate their prejudices from their beliefs.

Such a re-examination of values by the individual usually occurs when a man or woman leaves adolescence and pro-gresses into the problems of mature living. A century and three-quarters is not long in the life of a nation which has grown as vigorously and violently as our own. We may well believe that our country is now coming into its majority, and that, as a man should do, it is trying to put away childish things. As the growing child begins to forget his toys, so we Americans may be overcoming our excessive admiration for our beautiful, efficient gadgetry.

All that is needed, to be sure, is a little better sense of proportion. An electric railroad in the attic is not much dif-ferent from a workshop in the basement. But to the boy his switches and tracks may be the most valuable possession in the world, while to the busy man his tools are simply a relaxing, healthy hobby.

As a defense or an escape from the hectic pace of modern living, a growing number of people seem to be turning to such simpler pleasures. For those whose enjoyment of their leisure is found in gardening or bird watching, skiing or hiking, col-lecting rocks or wildflowers or butterflies, it is hard to be seriously annoyed with the scientist probing some theoretical mystery or contradiction in space or matter. Such people can

148

hardly blame him for not being in the least concerned as to whether the answer he finds will have immediate utility or any final, practical value. In a very real sense the amateur who asserts a liking for some aspect of nature or of its sciences, purely for the added pleasure it gives him in living, is placing himself on the same plane of motivation as the scientist or mathematician who pursues new knowledge for its own sake.

On the level of mechanical marvels, the American meteorologist has an imposing variety, a magnificent array of instruments, devices and gadgets with which to measure and sample the atmosphere and all its manifestations. Carried upward by balloons, shot aloft by rockets, contraptions of the most concentrated complexity operate automatic cameras and robot radios.

Much as the amateur may admire their perfection, he is unable to understand their functions, and his knowledge is insufficient to appreciate their utility. The average man—trying to check the midnight forecast by the morning clouds or inquisitively observing one of the weather's eternal sequences at any time of day—is more closely attuned to pure science than to its most recent mechanical and electronic devices. As they were for scientists of two hundred years ago, the basic instruments will be enough for his simple purpose. These are the barometer, the thermometer and the weather vane. Or if these, indeed, are too mechanically fancy, his liver, a broken bone or a rheumatic twinge will record the atmosphere's pressure, his nose or cheek the temperature, while a moistened finger can always be raised to measure the force and direction of the wind.

II

At hundreds of stations across the United States refined and perfected instruments record precise data on the moving atmosphere and its shifting weather. Tabulated to a common time, corrected to a uniform base, this information is transmitted every six hours by teletype to the central office of the U. S. Weather Bureau in Washington. There it is incorporated in the nation's master map. This chart is then flashed back by telegraphic facsimile to all the original reporting stations.

It goes likewise to a wide variety of other interested people and organizations. Experts study each new map, relating its newest episodes to the narrative told by its predecessors. In harbors and naval stations, operations will be adjusted to what it indicates. At military fields and commercial airports, most of the day's activities will be governed by its story. For the Coast Guard, mother of small craft and guide to all coastal shipping, the events it may foretell will determine a large part of the day's work.

For others it has a more specialized, but equally close interest. To the men at the dams that help control the flow of our great rivers, deep snow in winter brings threat of springtime flood. They watch for the hot, unseasonable Chinook wind, for the sudden warm spell, for a great storm of rain, that they may open their floodgates in good time to provide a reservoir for the excess water flooding down in brooks and streams high above them.

To the engineers at the turbines and dynamos that send current into our homes and offices, the passage of a severe cold front or the build-up of sudden thunderstorm can cause the flipping of a million switches. A cold rain and a falling temperature may require the services of a thousand maintenance crews as the crackling ice begins to build up on tree and bush and power line.

But for the busy man in the street and his equally busy wife, the weather map serves principally as a necessary means to an oversimple end. It is the basis for the forecast which he reads in his paper or which she hears at the end of some radio broadcast of the news. All the expensive and complicated instruments, the information flashed back and forth across the nation, the trained and educated personnel pitting their knowledge and skill against the weather's imponderables, all end up, for most of us, as a capsule statement, such as, "fair and warmer" or "cloudy with occasional showers."

This is essentially a nonsensical situation, doing little credit either to the age or country in which we live. Over an area usually several hundred miles across, the weather man is expected to tell us unerringly the expected high and low temperature, the winds and clouds to be anticipated, the extent and kind of any probable precipitation, as well as the time and duration of its occurrence. And all this must be compressed, since we are in such a rushing hurry, into about the number of words allowed in a standard telegram.

Essentially every such prediction is no more than a well-substantiated estimate, a highly educated guess. With a little knowledge and his five senses, the interested layman can have a lot of fun observing how accurately each forecast is working out. With only the simplest instruments, sportsman and businessman alike can derive solid advantage from adjusting the weather man's original prophesy by the actual conditions as they later appear.

To human planning, the moving weather presents the initial question of when. In our day-to-day affairs we wish to know, for example, when an expected cold front will strike, or when the falling rain will stop. Unless each occurs when predicted, a Sunday's picnic may be spoiled or a week-end expedition necessarily postponed.

In such plans the amateur can make his own forecast by observing the weather's actual timing and then comparing it with what the weather man predicted many hours earlier. Whether a meteorological event is early or late is in itself an important clue to what will follow after. When beneath a leaden sky, for example, the clouds do not lift and the rains stop as predicted, it is probable that a storm is receiving new supplies of water vapor and that the air aloft is co-operating in its continuing expansion. Since these atmospheric whirlpools must proceed to their natural climax, the arrival of such unforeseen reinforcements is assurance of no early break in the dampening prospect.

When a front and its system of clouds arrives upon the scene ahead of schedule, this is a clear indication that the forces involved are growing in strength. In the case of a warm front, the clouds will be thicker, the rainfall heavier and the air following its passage will be warmer and wetter than previously expected. If it is a cold front that looms up on the horizon well ahead of time, the frontal line of squalls and turbulence will be more powerful, the northern winds will blow more strongly and the temperature in due time will drop lower than was earlier thought likely by the Weather Bureau.

If, on the other hand, the arrival of a front is delayed, it is evidence that the original contrast between the two air masses is decreasing, that the meteorological battle is tending toward a stalemate and that the weather may, in fact, stagnate. Sometimes under such circumstances of diminishing difference, new atmospheric conditions can come into existence, setting off a totally unexpected set of future developments which then can be evaluated, by amateur and professional alike, only as they occur.

III

For the layman the harbingers of weather are the winds and the clouds. The high cirrus, for example, is produced in atmospheric currents which have moved throughout the whole depth of the troposphere. When its lovely plumes and streaks thin out and clear away, it is an excellent sign of improving weather. But if it thickens and in due course lowers while the clouds of the middle levels appear, a deepening disturbance is certainly approaching.

The winds will tell you where such a storm is centered. Facing them in our hemisphere, your right hand, pointing out and a little behind you, will indicate its focus. If instead it is a center of high pressure and its good weather one wishes to locate, a similarly raised left hand will indicate its approximate position.

In winter it is particularly useful to know if a storm's center will pass to the north or the south. The northern sector will produce a heavy fall of snow that may delight the skier but will plague the suburban and city dweller. When the storm passes to the north, however, the warm southern front's passage will usually turn the snow into rain and melt off much of the white blanket that has previously fallen.

In the story of the weather a chain of such events is sensibly called a *sequence*. An increase in the size of the raindrops or the snowflakes is part of the sequence which usually indicates that a front is drawing nearer. If this change occurs slowly and steadily, accompanied by a rise in the thermometer, it is a sign that it is a warm front which is approaching. If, however, these events are then followed by sudden heavy rain and a drop in the temperature, the passage is that of an occluded front, the atmospheric arrangement in which a great bulge of cold air has overtaken and lifted the warmer air mass from the south.

Such is the clearing shower that often foretells the cessation of the rain. But there is really nothing certain and sure about the weather's behavior. In a severe and deepening depression such showers along an extended occluded front may occur again and again, as fresh moisture-laden air swirls in against the almost stationary cold shoulder of the forces of the north.

The wind can tell you a lot about how such fronts are moving. If the easterly surface winds swing around into the north or northwest, it is a good sign that such an occluded front has finally moved past. If, however, the air's currents change to blow from the south or southwest, as the rain ends, you may be sure a warm air mass has taken possession of the air space directly above you.

From the official forecast or the last weather map, you will know whether a cold front is then likely to follow. If and when such a frontal line with its characteristic sequences passes over, the amount of disturbance in cloud and turbulence will tell you much about the contrast between the two conflicting air masses. The direction into which the wind then changes will strongly indicate the characteristics of the new mass of air which has moved over your locality. The more northerly and strong the wind, the colder and clearer will generally be the subsequent weather.

A cold front may at times develop along its length some kink in which the air begins to eddy. Into this, particularly along the Gulf of Mexico or the Atlantic coast, moist air may start to flow off the water. If, as a cold front is passing over you, you find the wind going back into the east instead of changing, as it should, into the north or west, you must be prepared for an unexpected worsening in the weather.

Apart from its behavior at such frontal lines, the circling winds move with the vagrant masses of the atmosphere. In our latitudes these come to us predominantly out of the west. Rooted to one spot, we human observers see this process as a change in the speed and direction of the wind.

Closely coupled with these changes moves the mercury in Torricelli's tube. A rise in the thermometer and an increase in the air's humidity tends to lighten the atmospheric load, while a shift to colder, drier air acts to increase it. In general, therefore, the barometer stands higher in winter than it does in summer, lower during the day than during the night. Yet these adjustments represent more or less errant shifts in this instrument's level as compared to the major changes which accompany the dynamic motion of the air that we feel as wind.

As a mass of cool, dry, descending air approaches us, the barometer rises steadily, while the advancing winds blow strongly around its eastern rim. If its center is expected to pass close overhead, the forecast is then for the glass to steady, the winds to drop, and the weather to be clear and cool. Toward the center of a good-sized atmospheric depression, on the other hand, the winds rise in velocity. Therefore a falling barometer, accompanied by an increase in the wind, is excellent evidence that the weather will deteriorate.

A more complete estimate of the weather's future sequence is obtained by noting the way in which the wind is shifting. When the barometer says that an area of low pressure is moving in your direction, a weather vane, which turns slowly clockwise as the winds shift, tells you that the center will pass to the north of you, that the clouds when they clear away will probably be followed by warmer temperatures. A contrary or backing trend to the smoke from a chimney or to a flag on a pole indicates that the storm's focal point will pass to the southward and the rainy weather will be raw; the eventual clearing will be to colder conditions.

As the barometer rises, on the other hand, a veering wind, shifting around in a clockwise direction, informs the observer that the center of high pressure is apt to pass to the north of him. The expectation is then for rising temperature and clear skies. If instead the winds swing the other way, while the mercury stays high in its glass, the prediction is colder with some increase in cloudiness.

The usual sequence in our weather is for successive regions of high and low pressure to follow each other across the map. But these are not always circular whirlpools in the atmosphere.

Often between two masses of cool descending air is thrust a valley of low pressure, called a *trough*. Or, separating two cyclonic storms, a long area of high barometric readings appears, termed a *ridge*. Here, in both cases, the winds die down as the edge of the first turntable of air passes over. Then as the wind starts to blow again from approximately the opposite direction, the barometer reverses its trend and the second rotating mass takes possession of the space above you.

Guided by such shifts in the direction and velocity of the surface winds, noting how the clouds are moving and changing aloft, with the barometer's rise and fall to suggest what is happening throughout the depth of the atmosphere, it is usually not hard to deduce how the weather man's forecast is working out and how it should be adjusted by what is observably happening in the air above us.

Such observation of the weather's progress will greatly improve the useful results to be obtained from the millions of dollars the taxpayers spend on the Weather Bureau and its expert facilities. For farmers and sportsmen, housewives and businessmen, this knowledge will improve their professional competence, the ability to handle each his daily job. And yet possibly of all things most important there is the enjoyment of life in the natural setting of our environment. Here perhaps is the best plea for the attainment of the elementary knowledge necessary to observe and predict the weather in its endless sequence.

IV

To the island residents who live where the hurricane strikes, the signs that portend its arrival are well and fearfully known. In Kansas and elsewhere along the flat lands of the Mississippi's basin the native folk apprehend and recognize the meteorological conditions from which the twister or tornado may spring. In many other parts of the world certain moods of the weather bring danger or discomfort. By familiarity the denizens of these localities learn the indications which forecast such on-coming.

To most of us in the United States the hazards of the weather are more trivial, their incidence only infrequently anything but merely inconvenient. Yet every winter, in ice storm or blizzard, quantities of cars are stalled, a good number wrecked and a few of their drivers killed. Each summer, too, many of our citizens and their children are drowned or struck by lightning when a summer storm comes up unexpectedly.

To the man who must go about his work in all weathers, to the doctor or seaman, for example, these are the minor dangers of his profession or trade. But to many another his automobile is just a more convenient mode of transportation than the train; his day on the water a pleasant way to get himself and his family a healthy dose of sun and fresh air.

The summer thunderstorm is probably the most serious threat as measured by actual loss of life. But the conditions from which it springs are easy enough to diagnose, its dangers not overly difficult to avoid. It is almost childishly obvious that the tree which may furnish partial shelter from the sudden rain is at the same time the likeliest target for the lightning's bolt. It is equally clear that the terrible turbulence within the tumbling clouds can reach down and set up sudden, violent squalls perfectly designed to work havoc among the small craft dotting lake, bay or sound.

Ice storm and blizzard occur as part of the sequence of a whirling, cyclonic storm. Cold air at the surface, to freeze the rain falling out of warmer levels aloft, causes the first. Especially plentiful sources of water vapor feeding into a storm's northern semicircle is generally what produces the second. The meteorological results usually stretch over a wide area. But the thunderstorm often strikes erratically, when it occurs. The sun may well be shining in one spot, while only a few miles away the wind will be tearing at the treetops, and hailstones will be rattling on the ground.

That there are two types of thunderstorm is the first fact for vacationer, week-ender or Sunday driver to appreciate. The first is the individual, self-contained disturbance occurring usually within a warm air mass. It occurs only in summer, generally towards late afternoon when the earth's surface becomes hottest. The second is the kind that forms along the rolling edge of a strong cold front. This latter, which may take place any time in the year, can produce the anomaly of thunder and lightning in the dead of a winter's night.

Occasionally the two can occur together when a cold front moves in during a summer afternoon, upon a hot, muggy air mass in which the congested cumulus is already towering high overhead. This is by far the most dangerous situation, since the winds may then form a continuous line of squalls that sweep a long sickle of wicked violence across land and water.

Thunderstorms are bred in air that is warm and wet. As the clouds billow up beneath the sun's warming rays they benefit from a degree of stillness in the upper and lower air. Strong, steady winds interrupt and prevent the vertical currents from forming around centers of concentrated congestion. In time, to be sure, the turbulent currents will produce their own eddies and gusts, but a hazy, hot, humid morning provides clear portent of thunder and lightning for the afternoon.

In such individual storms the bolts flash not only from cloud to cloud but generally, too, from the sky earthwards and from the earth skywards. Along a cold front, however, the condensation level is usually so high that most of the electric discharges cannot reach down to the surface. When, however, the thunder's clap sounds close behind the lightning's flash, it is best to be under some shelter that thrusts no beckoning finger skyward, unless it be made of steel or iron which will conduct the charge harmlessly in the direction it is determined to go. For this purpose the modern automobile is close to ideal.

Many a cold front, the weather-wise will note, is not really cold, particularly in late summer. The difference between the air behind it and that in its path may be largely in their relative humidities. Dry warm air, bulging or running over wet air at about the same temperature, is the situation out of which the hurricane is believed to grow and from which it is known the western tornado strikes.

On a smaller scale this same condition is most to be feared at lake or seacoast. If a line of heavily shaded clouds begins to rise above the western horizon, while all around you tower the individual masses of cumulus congestus, the time has come to row promptly to shore, to seek quickly some sheltered anchorage or to pack up the picnic things and collect your party. If, however, these steps are not possible, one must prepare one's self and one's companions for an experience which may well be thrilling, but which at times will be highly dangerous.

V

Usually the predictions of the Weather Bureau are closely accurate and easy to follow. Less frequently the forecast will have some element of uncertainty in it, as to direction or timing, for example, which the amateur will have little difficulty in appreciating and for which he will make his own local adjustments. But occasionally the shifting troposphere seems to violate all its own rules, to move and act in a way totally incomprehensible to expert and layman alike.

On April 12, 1952, the weather map that was drawn as of 1:30 A.M. showed a large area of high pressure centered northwest of Buffalo and a smaller region of low pressure

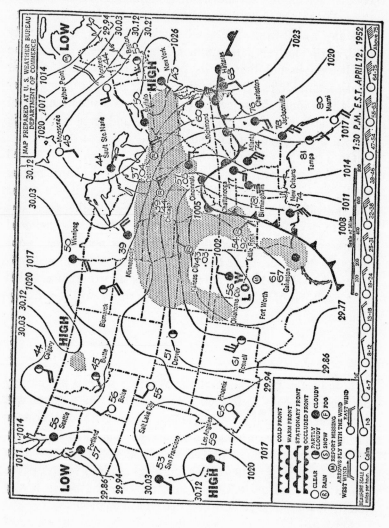

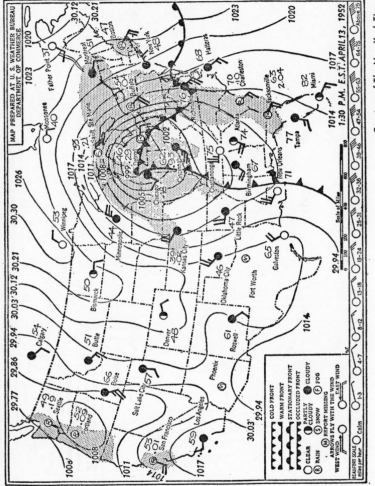

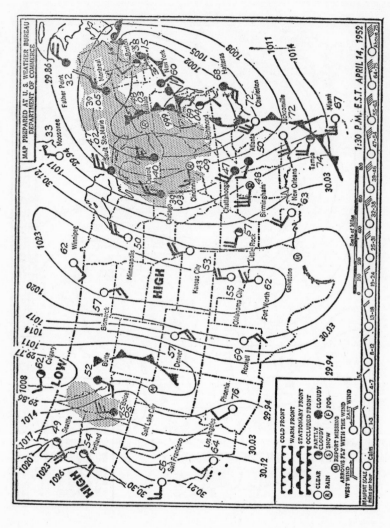

Courtesy of The New York Times

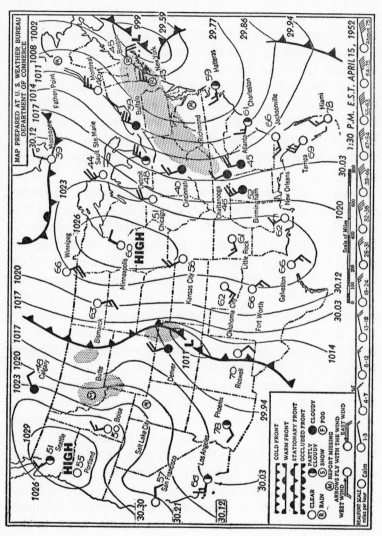

above the panhandle of Texas. Northeastward, over Oklahoma, Kansas, Missouri and Iowa, rain was falling. South of these states warm air from the Gulf followed northward over a long frontal line stretching in a shallow S across the southern states.

Twelve hours later, on the first map illustrated herein, this sweeping front had changed into an inverted U, while the area of rain had thrust a broad nose rapidly eastward, below the Great Lakes across the Alleghanies, all the way to the Delaware River. Into the bulging warm front over eastern Kentucky, strong winds above Mississippi, Alabama and Georgia were carrying a deep current of warm wet air northward.

Despite this wide extension of the precipitation, the center of low pressure had moved only a short distance, and on this lunchtime map of April 12th, was situated over Oklahoma. Lying well to the west of the curving front, its connection therewith was high overhead, as the southern winds swept upwards and towards their left. Clearly, forces were loose which were building up an area of crowding isobars, cyclonic winds and deepening atmospheric depression. To the weather man this was all obvious enough, but he was required to predict the direction that the disturbance would take, the new regions into which the mounting storm would move.

Under the circumstances the question was difficult. Like the low far to the southwest, the high pressure center north of Buffalo was practically stationary. In spite of the increasing intensity of the atmospheric activity in between, the low to the south and the high to the north gave little indication of what they meant to do or where they intended to go.

Such indeterminate meteorological situations are not uncommon. In spite of his charts and instruments, his formulas and his higher mathematics, it is the weather itself, in the last analysis, that foretells for him its own future. In this case, however, the period of doubt was quickly ended. As the next map shows, the weather's picture promptly assumed a more normal typical pattern. By 1:30 in the afternoon of April 13th, the high pressure area had moved up the St. Lawrence and was out to sea. The bulging frontal line had adjusted itself to a cold front to the west running north and south, with a largely stationary front ahead of it to the northeast. The low pressure center had suddenly and rapidly moved northward and assumed its proper position above the spot where the two fronts came together in a point.

After such a dynamic readjustment, the clear likelihood was that the now typical extratropical cyclone would advance determinedly eastward. Urged on by the high above Winnipeg, it should be out to sea in another day or day and a half. New York, Pennsylvania and New Jersey, which had now suffered through two days of rain, should probably be enjoying clearing weather within twenty-four hours.

Frustratingly enough, the storm refused to follow a normal sequence. As of 1:30 P.M. on the 14th, its center had advanced only into western New York. After its quick spurt northward, the air ahead of it was now refusing it quick access to the sea; the winds behind it were unable to urge it vigorously onward. On this new map, too, the high moving down out of Canada had assumed a distinctly unusual pattern. Instead of forming a circling wheel, the air from the north had become a lozenge-shaped ridge, running in a great crescent from the Canadian border to the Gulf of Mexico. On its northeast edge, air from Greenland and the northern waters was sweeping southwestward in deep, strong currents into the northern sector of the now slowly moving disturbance.

Twenty-four hours later the storm at last had moved out to sea. Centered somewhere to the south of Nantucket and its shoals, its slow progress thereto was shown by the map of 1:30 P.M. on April 15th. Behind it the high pressure ridge had moved an even lesser distance. Yet in a narrow belt

165

running northeastward, from the mountains of Kentucky, across Pennsylvania and into southern New England, the rain still fell, and the clouds lay, low and heavy, where the cold wet winds from the Icelandic low continued to blow southward strongly in converging currents.

Finally by the next day the rain stopped and the clouds cleared away. But altogether it had been a bad four or five days for the weather man. During that period the air had for a time moved throughout its whole depth in wide, curving currents. In this action the atmosphere was no doubt redressing some severe unbalance in its pressure or distribution. But with all his scientific knowledge, despite all his probings and calculations, man does not know what produces such great surgings or how to predict their outcome.

If meteorology were an exact science, there would be little need to go behind the predictions made daily by the Weather Bureau. But as things are, and as they will most likely remain for some time to come, you and I can wisely, usefully and enjoyably acquire some working knowledge of the doubts and difficulties that on occasion assault the expert.

For some, to be sure, the simple position of the Vermont guide may be adequate. After three wet, miserable days in camp, one of his party asked him if it would ever stop raining. His answer, based on a lifetime's experience, was undeniable: "It always has."

For most of us, however, the rewards of some weather wisdom will be considerable. There will be, first, the pleasure of second-guessing the expert. Next, as we work or play, our knowledge will pay us useful dividends. Last, and perhaps best of all, we will recapture a closer contact with the inherited recollections, which in the animals we call instinct, handed down to us through the centuries, from the time when our ancestors peered anxiously at the skies as they hunted, fished or engaged in savage tribal warfare.

Glossary

ATMOSPHERE: The gaseous envelope of any celestial body.

COLD FRONT: A frontal surface, rising and curving upward from the ground, which is formed when cold air is moving forward and pushing warm air out of its path.

COLD POLE: That spot on the earth's surface where the coldest temperatures are registered. The north cold pole is situated in northern Siberia.

CONDENSATION LEVEL: The height above the ground at which a given parcel of air will reach the dew point, where its water vapor will condense or sublime into cloud.

CONTINENTAL: The adjective describing a mass of air which has acquired its properties over a large expanse of land. It likewise describes the climate that is characteristic of the continents.

CORIOLUS: The apparent force, arising out of the earth's rotation and its spherical shape, which causes all objects moving parallel to the earth's surface to be deflected to the right in the northern, to the left in the southern hemisphere. Its intensity varies with latitude and the velocity of the moving object.

CYCLONE: A horizontal vortex in the troposphere rotating counterclockwise in the northern hemisphere, clockwise in the southern. It is an area of low atmospheric pressure. Its opposite is an anticyclone.

DEPRESSION: An area of low atmospheric pressure.

DEW POINT: The temperature to which any given parcel of air must be cooled in order to raise its humidity to 100 per cent.

EQUATORIAL FRONT: A frontal surface characterized by high cumulus clouds, often accompanied by thunderstorms and extreme turbulence. It arises when air from north and south of the equator moves down into direct collision.

EXTRATROPICAL CYCLONE: The circular storm of the middle latitudes; occurring, that is, outside of the tropics. They arise out of differences between two or more masses of air and are therefore characterized by unsymmetrical discontinuities at the frontal surfaces.

FREEZING LEVEL: The height above the ground at which fresh water would freeze. Clouds, however, consisting of liquid droplets are sometimes found whose temperatures are below that of freezing. Such clouds are termed *supercooled*.

FRONT: A surface in the atmosphere, stretching from the earth's surface up into the troposphere, which divides two bodies of dissimilar or contrasting air.

HIGH: An abbreviation for an area of high barometric pressure.

HUMIDITY: The measure of the amount of water vapor in a given parcel of air. Usually given relative to saturated air, as the relative humidity in percentage.

HURRICANE: The name given to a tropical cyclone in the western Atlantic Ocean. Its derivation is assigned to a Carib Indian word for a big storm.

INVERSION: A level in the troposphere where the usual decrease of temperature with altitude is reversed. A level, therefore, that is as warm or warmer than the one below it. An inversion resists or prevents the further ascent of vertical currents.

ISOBAR: A line passing through a series of points on the earth's surface all of which record the same barometric pressure. In the measurement of such pressure, all readings are adjusted to that at sea level.

JET STREAM: A swift current in the air of the upper troposphere and lower stratosphere. Undulating over a cycle of four to six weeks, its average position is over the 45th parallel of latitude.

LOW: An abbreviation for an area of low barometric pressure.

MARITIME: The adjective describing air that has acquired its properties over a large expanse of ocean. It likewise describes the climate characteristic of the oceans.

METEOROLOGY: As usually used, the science that deals with the weather. In general it is the science that is concerned with the whole of the earth's atmosphere.

NUCLEI: Dust showing an affinity for water acts as nuclei for the change of water vapor into the droplets or ice crystals forming cloud. Those particles which dissolve in this process are termed *condensation nuclei*; those that do not are called *sublimation nuclei*.

OCCLUDED FRONT: A combination of two frontal surfaces, in which one surface rests upon the ground and the other rests aloft against the first. In the United States it is generally a *cold front* which lifts a *warm front,* but elsewhere a *warm front* is sometimes found lifting a *cold front*.

OXYGEN: The eighth element in the atomic table. Two atoms of this element form the gas of the same name, which comprises approximately one fifth of the earth's atmosphere.

OZONE: A blue gas with a strong odor, each of whose molecules consist of three atoms of oxygen. At the earth's surface it is formed in an electric discharge, such as a stroke of lightning. In the stratosphere it is believed to be formed continuously by the action of certain highly penetrating rays of the sun.

POLAR FRONT: The surface reaching up into the troposphere where the prevailing westerlies meet the polar easterlies. On the earth the polar front shifts with the seasons back and forth across the 60th parallel of latitude.

RIDGE: An area of high barometric pressure which is longer than it is wide and hence shaped like a ridge. It often lies between two circular areas of low pressure.

SATURATION: In the atmosphere the state of balance when as many molecules of water vapor are leaving the air and returning to any wet surface as are entering the air by evaporation.

STABLE AIR: When the levels of the troposphere grow colder with altitude at less than 3° F for each 1000 feet, they are called *stable,* since this rate resists or prevents the ascent of vertical currents.

STRATOSPHERE: That portion of the earth's atmosphere which lies beyond the troposphere. Its depth is approximately fifty miles. It is characterized by a uniformity of temperature, which is believed to result from the absorption of solar energy by ozone.

SUBLIMATION: The change of a gas directly into its solid state. In the atmosphere the change of water vapor into ice crystals.

SUPERIOR AIR: A mass of air from the upper troposphere, which sinks down as a whole to the earth's surface, retaining its property of extreme dryness.

SUPERCOOLED: A state of unbalance analogous to supersaturation. Water can be cooled to below its normal freezing temperature if it is absolutely pure and is not jarred or vibrated. Clouds in this condition are termed *supercooled*.

SUPERSATURATION: In the atmosphere the state of unbalance arising when a parcel of air is above 100 per cent humidity. This condition arises when there is an absence of the usual dust on which the water vapor otherwise can adhere in changing to its liquid or solid state.

TROPICS: The tropics are circles of latitude on the earth's surface. They mark the limits at which the sun can be seen directly overhead at midday. The Tropic of Cancer is at 28° 17′ north latitude, the Tropic of Capricorn at the same position in south latitude.

TROPICAL CYCLONE: The circular storms originating within the tropics, which are caused by the piercing of the *trade wind inversion*. Their pattern as a result is predominantly symmetrical.

TROPOSPHERE: That portion of the atmosphere lying next to the earth's surface. In it the temperature decreases on the average with altitude. Its depth ranges from nine to ten miles at the equator, from five to six miles over the Poles.

TROUGH: An area of low barometric pressure which is longer than it is wide and hence shaped like a trough. It often lies between two circular areas of high pressure.

UNSTABLE AIR: When the levels of the troposphere grow colder with altitude at more than 3° F for each 1000 feet, they are called unstable. At a rate between 3° and 5½° F per 1000 feet, such air is termed *conditionally unstable,* since clouds must form to assist any rising thermal current. At a rate above 5½° F the air is called *absolutely unstable,* since any heated parcel of air will continue rising through such levels.

WARM FRONT: A frontal surface, shaped like a long ramp, which is formed when warm air is advancing along the ground and pushing cold air ahead of it.

WATER VAPOR: The gaseous form of water, when below the boiling point. Above this point such gas is called steam.

WAVE: A small bend or undulation in a stationary front, from which may develop an extratropical cyclone.

Index

Absolutely unstable air, 18
Afghanistan, 43
Air-mass clouds, 75
Alaska, 46
Aleutian Islands, 41, 42, 95
Aleutian low, 42, 48, 58, 104
Alps, 43
Altitude, clouds grouped by, 82-83; maps, 135-36
Altocumulus clouds, 73-74, 82, 83
Altostratus clouds, 73-74, 82, 83, 121
Amazon River, 59
Andes mountains, 43, 59
Antarctica, 42, 118, 121
Arabian Desert, 28, 60
Arctic air mass, 58
Arctic Circle, 25, 48, 49, 69, 111
Arctic Sea, 36
Argentina, 59
Asia, continental climate, 45-46
Atmosphere, 3-19, 167
Atomic power, 98-100, 147
Australia, 37, 43, 60, 118, 122
Axis of earth, 32-33, 69
Azores, 48

Barometer, 87, 88, 89, 90, 92, 94-95, 96, 108, 123, 132, 149, 154, 155, 156

Bay of Bengal, 5
Beaufort scale, 135
Becquerel, 38, 99, 100
Bering Sea, 31, 43, 59
Bermuda, 48, 66
Bermuda high, 42, 122
Bjerknes, 52, 57, 132, 148
Blizzards, 157
Borneo, 45
Bowditch, Nathaniel, 5
Brazil, 59
Burma, 44

Canada, 48, 70, 72
Cape of Good Hope, 50, 118
Caribbean Islands, 21, 123
Cartography, 127-29
Caucasian race, 28
Center of storm, 153-56
Ceylon, 45
Charts, 108-9, 127-46
Children's Crusade, 47
Chile, 43
China, 44, 45
Christmas Island, 120-21
Cirrocumulus clouds, 74-75, 82, 83
Cirrostratus clouds, 74, 83
Cirrus clouds, 74, 83, 121
Climate, cycle, 33

INDEX

Clipper ships, 20-21

Clouds, air-mass, 75; altitude groupings, 82-83; altocumulus, 73-74, 82, 83; altostratus, 73-74, 82, 83, 121; changeability, 82; cirrocumulus, 74-75, 82, 83; cirrostratus, 74, 83; cirrus, 74, 83, 121; cumulonimbus, 77, 82; cumulus, 16, 17, 19, 70, 71, 75-79, 80, 95, 120, 121; cumulus congestus, 76-79, 82, 159; cumulus humilis, 76, 82; fair weather cumulus, 76, 80, 82, 122, 125; nimbostratus, 81, 83; stratocumulus, 73, 83; stratus, 70, 73, 79, 80, 81, 82, 83, 95

Coast Guard, U. S., 51

Cold front, 55-56, 78, 109, 132, 154, 158, 159, 167

Cold pole, 44, 167

Columbus, Christopher, 21

Condensation level, 167

Condensation nuclei, 14, 169

Conditionally unstable air, 18

Conflicting air masses, theory of, 52, 57, 130, 132

Congested cumulus clouds, 76-79, 82, 122, 125, 159

Continental air mass, 58, 133, 167

Continental drift, 37, 68, 113-18

Conventional signs, 128-29

Coriolus, 22, 23, 90, 93, 109, 167

Cumulonimbus clouds, 77, 82

Cumulus clouds, 16, 17, 19, 70, 71, 75-79, 80, 95, 120, 121

Cumulus congestus clouds, 76-77, 82, 122, 125, 159

Cumulus humilis clouds, 76, 82

Cumulus rain-cloud, 77

Curie, Marie and Pierre, 38, 99-100

Cyclonic storm, 60-64, 94-95, 122, 157, 167

Deflection, 89-90, 93-94, 109

Depression, 131, 167

Dew point, 11, 79, 167

Doldrums, 21, 24, 31, 33, 118, 121

Dust, atmospheric, 7, 11-15, 71, 72, 73, 75

Einstein, Albert, 147

Equator, 88, 103, 104, 120, 121, 122, 124

Equatorial air mass, 58

Equatorial front, 168

Equatorial weather, 119-26

Evaporation, 9

Extratropical cyclones, 60-61, 64, 165, 168

Fair weather cumulus clouds, 76, 80, 82, 122, 125

Fog, 42, 58, 79-81, 137

Forecasting, weather, 50, 105, 112, 119, 126, 130, 132, 138-46, 159

Freezing level, 168

Front, 132, 168; see also Cold front; Equatorial front; Occluded front; Polar front; Stationary front; Warm front

Frontal zones, 57

Galileo, 32, 85, 114, 115

Galvani, 98

Garden of Eden, 27, 39

Genghis Khan, 47

Geodesy, 114

Gibraltar, 50

Gobi Desert, 28, 44, 60

Goodyear, 98

Grand Banks, 80

Greenland, 45, 51, 113, 114

Guam, 101

Gulf of Mexico, 48, 58, 79, 134, 154

Gulf Stream, 35, 40, 42, 67, 70, 80

Hail, 78, 158

Halsey, Admiral, 119

Hang-Ho River, 45

Hawaiian Islands, 48, 120
Heat, 9, 15-19, 40, 84, 95
High, defined, 131, 168
High pressure areas, 42
Himalaya mountains, 43
Horizontal circulation, 70, 71, 89
Horse latitudes, 27-28, 31, 41, 48, 69, 89, 103, 121, 125
Hudson Bay, 48
Humidity, 10-12, 168
Hurricanes, tropical, 64-67, 79, 95-96, 122-26, 156-57, 159, 168
Hydrographic Office, Navy's, 119

Ice Age, 39, 72
Icebergs, 51
Ice crystals, formation, 72, 77, 81, 82, 83
Iceland, 41, 42, 95
Icelandic low, 42, 48, 58, 104, 166
Ice storms, 55, 157
India, 44, 45, 60
Indian Ocean, 5, 60, 122
Inversion, 168
Isobars, 130-31, 133, 137, 168
Isostasy, 116

Japanese Current, 40, 42
Jet stream, 100-103, 104-106, 139, 168

Kon-Tiki, 31
Korea, 60
Krakatau, 13

Labrador Current, 51, 80
Landmarks, terrestial, 114
Lift of continents, 68-69, 71
Lightning, 77, 79, 157, 158
Lincoln, Abraham, 47
Low, defined, 168
Low pressure areas, 42

Malaya, 44
Map-making, 127-46

Maritime air mass, 58, 133, 168-69
Maritime supremacy, U. S., 5-6, 20-21
Maury, Matthew Fontaine, 5
McKay, Donald, 5
Mercator, 36
Meteorology, 5, 8, 47, 50, 52, 57, 72, 87, 107, 132, 166, 169
Mexico, 58
Microscope, invention, 86
Migrations, 29-31, 47
Mistral, 91
Mongolia, 43
Mongolian race, 29, 47
Monsoons, 45, 48, 59, 91, 101
Moon, formation, 33, 37, 117-18
Motion, 17
Mountains, effect on climate, 43-46, 95

Negroid race, 29
New Yorker magazine, 123
Nimbostratus clouds, 81, 83
Norsemen, explorations, 30-31
North Atlantic high, 58
North Pacific high, 42, 58, 120, 121
North Pole, 42, 45, 48, 69, 103
Norway, 52, 113, 114, 132
Nuclei, see Condensation nuclei; Sublimation nuclei

Occluded front, 65, 66-67, 133, 153, 169
Ocean currents, 69
Origins of man, 28-32
Oxygen, 7-8, 169
Ozone, 6, 169

Pacific Ocean, 33, 37, 59, 118, 120
Panama Canal, 42, 50
Peasants' Revolt, 47
Pendulum experiment, 93-94
Persia, 43
Philippine Islands, 45, 122

Phlogiston, 84
Polar air mass, 58
Polar Easterly winds, 24-26, 41-42, 91
Polar front, 52-53, 169
Polynesians, 6, 29, 31, 119
Precipitation, 81, 83, 137
Pressure, atmospheric, 9, 42, 84-85, 86-87, 92, 94, 95-96, 108, 155
Prevailing westerly winds, 26-28, 41, 91
Ptolemy, 32
Pyrenees, 43

Radio-sounding devices, 52
Rain making, 14-15, 81
Relative humidity, 10-12
Renaissance, 84-85
Ridge, 131, 156, 169
Roaring Forties, 5, 31
Rocky Mountains, 134
Röntgen, 98
Rotation of earth, 24, 33, 84, 93

Sahara Desert, 16, 28, 60, 91
Saturation, 169
Saturn, rings of, 117
Science, development, 84-87, 98-100, 113, 147-49
Scotland, 70
Seasonal cycle, 33-35, 46, 47-49, 104
Semitic race, 28
Sequence, 153
Shooting stars, 6
Siam, 44
Siberia, 44, 45, 46, 48, 72, 104
Silver iodide, 14-15, 81
Snow, 78, 81
Solar radiation, 6
Stable air, 18-19, 169
Static electricity, see Lightning
Stationary front, 57, 133
Steamship lanes, 50-51
Stratocumulus clouds, 73, 83

Stratosphere, 7, 88, 97, 103, 120, 170
Stratus clouds, 70, 73, 79, 80, 81, 82, 83, 95
Sublimation, defined, 170
Sublimation nuclei, 14, 72, 169
Sunda Straits, 5
Supercooled, 170
Superior air, 125, 134, 170
Supersaturation, 170
Symbols, map-making, 128-29, 133-34, 135, 137

Telescope, invention, 85-86
Temperature, 136
Texas, 79
Thermometer, 149, 154
Thorium, 38
Thunder, 77, 158
Thunderhead, 70, 77, 78, 157, 158-59
Thunderstorms, see Thunderhead
Tidal wave, 123
Tides, 24, 123
Titanic, 51
Topographical map, 130
Tornado, 159
Torricelli, 85, 86, 87, 94
Torricelli's tube, see Barometer
Trade winds, 21-24, 31, 33, 41, 48, 51, 91, 118, 119, 121
Tropical air mass, 58
Tropical cyclone, 94-95, 170
Tropical hurricanes, 64-67, 79, 95-96, 122-26, 156-57, 159
Tropics, defined, 170
Troposphere, 8, 27, 49, 82, 83, 88, 91, 100-6, 107-12, 120, 125, 159, 170
Trough, 131, 156, 170
Turkey, 43
Typhoons, see Tropical hurricanes

United States, maritime supremacy, 5-6, 20-21
Unstable air, 18-19, 170-71

Upper air, behavior, 100-106, 107-12
Ural mountains, 43
Uranium, 38, 99

Vandal migrations, 47
Vertical circulation, 69-70, 71, 72, 88, 89
Volcanic dust, 13

Warm front, 55, 56, 109, 132, 153, 171
Waterspouts, 122
Water vapor, 6, 9-11, 95, 123, 171
Wave, 171
Weather Bureau, U. S., 102, 159, 166

Weather planes, 102, 125-26
Weather ships, 51, 103
Weather vane, 149, 155
Willi-willies, 122
Winds, jet stream, 100-103; mistral, 91; monsoons, 45, 48, 59, 91, 101; Polar easterlies, 24-26, 41-42, 91; Prevailing Westerlies, 26-28, 41, 91; trade, 21-24, 31, 33, 41, 48, 51, 91, 118, 119, 121

X-ray discovery, 98

Yangtse River, 45

Code Number	C_L	CLOUDS, LOW — Description (Abridged From W.M.O. Code)
1		Cu with little vertical development and seemingly flattened.
2		Cu of considerable development, generally towering, with or without other Cu or Sc bases all at same level.
3		Cb with tops lacking clear-cut outlines, but distinctly not cirriform or anvil-shaped; with or without Cu, Sc, or St.
4		Sc formed by spreading out of Cu; Cu often present also.
5		Sc not formed by spreading out of Cu.
6		St or Fs or both, but not Fs of bad weather.
7		Fs and/or Fc of bad weather (scud) usually under As and Ns.
8		Cu and Sc (not formed by spreading out of Cu) with bases at different levels.
9		Cb having a clearly fibrous (cirriform) top, often anvil-shaped, with or without Cu, Sc, St, or scud.

Code Number	C_M	CLOUDS, MIDDLE — Description (Abridged From W.M.O. Code)
1		Thin As (entire cloud layer semitransparent).
2		Thick As, or Ns.
3		Thin Ac; cloud elements not changing much and at a single level.
4		Thin Ac in patches; cloud elements continually changing and/or occurring at more than one level.
5		Thin Ac in bands or in a layer gradually spreading over sky and usually thickening as a whole.
6		Ac formed by the spreading out of Cu.
7		Double-layered Ac or a thick layer of not increasing; or As and Ac both present at same or different levels.
8		Ac in the form of Cu-shaped tufts or with turrets.
9		Ac of a chaotic sky, usually at different levels; patches of dense Ci are usually present also.

Code Number	C_H	CLOUDS, HIGH — Description (Abridged From W.M.O. Code)
1		Filaments of Ci, scattered and not increasing.
2		Dense Ci in patches or twisted sheaves, usually not increasing.
3		Ci, often anvil-shaped, derived from or associated with Cb.
4		Ci, often hook-shaped, gradually spreading over the sky and usually thickening as a whole.
5		Ci and Cs, often in converging bands, or Cs alone; the continuous layer not reaching 45° altitude.
6		Ci and Cs, often in converging bands, or Cs alone; the continuous layer exceeding 45° altitude.
7		Cs covering the entire sky.
8		Cs not increasing and not covering entire sky; Ci and Cc may be present.
9		Cc alone or Cc with some Ci or Cs, but the Cc being the main cirriform cloud present.

Cloud Abbreviation
St or Fs-Stratus or Fractostratus
Ci-Cirrus
Cs-Cirrostratus
Cc-Cirrocumulus
Ac-Altocumulus
As-Altostratus
Sc-Stratocumulus
Ns-Nimbostratus
Cu or Fc-Cumulus or Fractocumulus
Cb-Cumulonimbus

Code Number	D_C	Cloud Direction
0	NONE	No Clouds or Calm
1		Northeast
2		East
3		Southeast
4		South
5		Southwest
6		West
7		Northwest
8		North
9	NONE	Unknown, Variable